The Mahabharata
Re-imagined

A collection of scenes from the Epic

The Mahabharata Re-imagined

A collection of scenes from the Epic

Trisha Das

Rupa & Co

Published in 2009 by

Rupa.Co

7/16, Ansari Road, Daryaganj,
New Delhi 110 002

Sales Centres:
Allahabad Bengalooru Chandigarh Chennai
Hyderabad Jaipur Kathmandu
Kolkata Mumbai

Typeset in Adobe Caslon by
Mindways Design
1410 Chiranjiv Tower,
43 Nehru Place
New Delhi 110 019

Printed in India by
Nutech Photolithographers
B-240, Okhla Industrial Area, Phase-I,
New Delhi 110 020, India

To Nanaji for firing the starter gun,
Ma & Poppy for cheering me on,
Deeps for running with me,
And Mr Rajiv Mehrotra for seeing me over the finish line.

CONTENTS

Draupadi's Initiation

Solid gold it was. Blinking from its intricate paisley surface, were bite-sized emeralds, rubies, pearls and, oddly enough, black sapphire, an addendum after the craftsman heard about the colour of her eyes. It rested easily on her head; a lifetime of wear had either shaped the crown or her skull into a good fit.

'Hold still, Princess Draupadi. Your *kohl* has smudged.'

The hand-maiden Neela, thin and wheat-coloured to Draupadi's dusky voluptuousness, leaned over her mistress's face and rubbed a rosewater-drenched cloth under her eye. The *kohl*, made this morning from char and almond oil by the loving hands of the hag Kesari, came away easily and stained the cloth. Neela dipped a careful finger into the black stain and with it, left a tiny mark on the side of Draupadi's forehead.

She smiled, 'You should never be perfect. Someone could get jealous and cast the evil eye upon you.'

Draupadi stood up, took a deep breath and tried to smile back. She failed. The attempt was belied by the quiver of her lips and incessant blink of her eye. Today, fear foiled the usual pride and courage in those flashes of black, bright like a gypsy fire in the desert out of a body almost buried in adornment.

A ring and chain of gold hung from her nose unto her lips and climbed her cheek to become lost in the red gossamer veil that fell over her forehead. Peeping out from it, an uncut ruby pendant, shaped like a new moon, hung between her eyebrows. Her thick hair, woven and piled with fragrant garlands of jasmine, was the royal crown's seat, her ears unseen under their gold twins. Gold bangles clinked on sleek, plump arms from which gold creepers stretched to clasp the base of each finger. A damp cleavage and a naked belly nestled under necklaces of precious stones, heaving from heat and anticipation. The small red cloth binding her bosom was partially hidden under a heavy red saree draped around Draupadi's body. Intricate embroidery with gold-plated silver thread weighed the silken cloth down around her, flattering her contours. Her delicate bare feet, encased in gold anklets and toe-rings shaped like lotuses, seemed almost unable to support the burden her small frame was carrying.

Draupadi stretched a hand towards her hand-maiden, 'Neela . . . .'

The large wooden door of her chambers, carved and painted in peacock blue-green, creaked, and a simply dressed serving girl slunk in carrying an earthen flask.

Draupadi didn't bother to look at her, 'Out!' She shouted. Her voice was sharp. The serving girl started, quickly bowed and slunk out of the room.

She took Neela's hand in her own and ran her soft fingers over the roughened palm, 'Ever since I can remember, you've rubbed sandalwood paste into my skin everyday to make it soft, yet never took care of your own.'

Neela shrugged and covered Draupadi's hand with her own, 'Remember your nemesis, the pumice stone? How you used to cry! But it worked, Princess. Not a hair dares grow on your body.' She laughed softly, 'I used to feel for you during those sessions. I was glad it was not me!'

Draupadi smiled distractedly, 'And I used to wish I was you. Anyway...' she said, after a moment, 'All these years, you've been my friend and sister. These last sixteen days, as we've looked out through those damned small windows at the amphitheatre day and night, you've been to me as you are to that minx who still suckles at your bosom even after two winters...a mother.'

There was a tear in Neela's eye, 'Princess...'

'No, let me finish,' Draupadi interrupted. 'I should ask you what you'll have in return for a lifetime of devotion and friendship. Instead, I have yet another behest. Will you come with me?'

Neela looked down.

Draupadi continued, 'My father can arrange for your man to be appointed as courtier in the palace of my future...husband,' she gulped and her lip quivered yet again, '...whoever he may be.'

Neela looked at her best friend, equal in age and superior in stature but junior in experience. So proud and regal was she, this daughter of a warrior king. This motherless girl, on the brink of womanhood, was about to realise her destiny. Nervous and vulnerable, yet her chin never bowed. 'I'll come with you.'

Draupadi nodded in satisfaction and squeezed Neela's hand as she often did when they were about to embark on some shared mission. Suddenly, there was a burst of deafening noise outside, as dozens of kettledrums started beating together in rhythm. Conches, loud and piercing, resounded in tune with the drums. People started cheering, thousands together and Draupadi could hear the mingled sounds of galloping horses, trumpeting elephants and giant wooden gates opening.

They looked at each other just as another hand-maiden, Saumya, burst into the room, panting. She looked at Draupadi and said in a rush, 'Krishna, King of the Vaishnavas, is here!

He has come with his brother, and rows upon rows of men bearing gifts. They say he's brought a hundred horses!'

Draupadi's face lit up as she felt expectant warmth fill her cheeks. She knew it. Krishna, whom she had adored from afar since she was a child, had come. To finally claim her hand, she thought happily. No better proof did she need that he loved her as she had always loved him.

'He has declined to be a contestant and will be attending as your father's guest of honour. The priests have lit the sacred fires. Your father has sent for you, Princess,' continued Saumya breathlessly, eyeing Draupadi carefully.

Draupadi felt the blush freeze in her cheeks as the stark slap of disappointment hit her. She opened her mouth to protest, in question, when Neela interrupted with a quelling look and nod in Saumya's direction, 'The time has come, Princess. Let us go.'

Draupadi nodded blankly but did not move. She felt her stomach churn as the extent of Krishna's rejection realised itself within her. Despite having playfully married herself to his carved image countless times in the privacy of her bedchambers, she would not marry him today. Tears stung her eyes even as she vainly tried to see her features.

Saumya continued, this time softly, sympathetically, 'Krishna has sent a message for you, Princess. He said to tell you not to be apprehensive. No ordinary man, even a king, can be your husband.'

Draupadi stared at Saumya stupidly for a moment and then straightened her spine. She desired Krishna's pity even less than she desired his rejection. She walked resolutely towards the doors. It was a bitter-sweet moment when she acknowledged that Krishna was right about one thing. Indeed, this day would ensure that no ordinary man, even a king, could be her husband.

✳

The guards, dressed for the occasion in red tunics with bright red turbans, parted as her entourage passed the palace halls and passages, their necks straining to catch a glimpse of the never before seen princess. First came the young children of the palace women, dressed in their finest, accompanied by their mothers. Then came the dancing eunuchs, dressed in bright cotton saris and silver jewellery, their bangles clanging as they clapped manly hands and shook saucy hips. The maidens followed, carrying the sacred water of the river Ganges and rose petals to sprinkle upon the floor before Draupadi could tread on it. They wore gilded saris in the colours of spring, their half-veiled faces teasing the eager audience of guards, soldiers and courtiers with views of un-kissed lips and secret eyes.

Then came Draupadi, flanked by Neela and the other hand-maidens. She walked slowly, carrying a golden platter with the traditional articles of prayer and an elaborate garland of the finest scented flowers. The guards noticed she was dark in complexion, unlike most royal women. Her head was held high, also unlike most women, who lowered their gaze under the scrutiny of men. Her beauty was not usual, full lips and high cheekbones belied the traditional. But, oh yes, she was beautiful, the guards agreed as she passed, leaving her signature scent of lotus flowers in the air. However, they decided, they would not like to own her. Under the shining skin and rippling skirts, they perceived intensity, a latent force not unlike the stiff, giant bow that rested at the centre of the amphitheatre.

✳

The marble floor felt soft and wet with the water and the petals left for her by her maidens. Draupadi noticed the walls of the grand rooms and hallways, their bright frescos and gold linings had been covered in garlands of orange and red marigold, each heavy door draped with leaves of the mango tree. Sunlight streamed in through the balconies, enclosures and inner courtyards, a light wind attending the occasion from the south-east. Unable to relish this happy portrait in her dejected state, Draupadi looked instead at the plate in her hands. The small, unlit oil lamp, red ochre, rice and sacred water in tiny bowls lay dormant, expectant. She would light the lamp before she faced her husband. She would sprinkle the water over him and apply the ochre and rice on his forehead with the third finger of her right hand. Apart from her father and brothers, she had never touched a man in her life. The thought that it would not be Krishna's smiling, handsome face she would touch, was almost too much to bear. She looked up with a jerk.

There was a faint scent of black aloe in the outside air, almost lost in the assorted odours of dung, humid sweat and smoky sandalwood incense. She left the palace door, shielded from the hot sun by a lackey with a silken umbrella, and sat in her *doli*, a shaded seat of cushions and gossamer curtains carried by four palace guards. Her entourage walked around her *doli* on a path of rose petals leading towards an imposing wooden amphitheatre shaded and draped by a pristine white canopy.

Neela stole her hand through the curtains and squeezed Draupadi's. She absently squeezed back even as her mind began to focus on the sight of the royal complex, unseen until this day. Through the curtains, she saw the lush palace grounds, crowded with horses, chariots and what seemed like thousands of people. There were groups of priests, costume-clad minstrels singing and dancing in front of dazzled villagers, hawkers selling their wares and people sitting around her path, waiting for a glimpse of their princess. From the amphitheatre came sounds of cheering, chanting and music and, once in every few moments, a man would run out of an arched entrance to shout the latest goings on inside. 'Prince Duryodhana, the bull, says he can do it with one hand behind his back!' 'They are saying the brothers, Sankha and Uttara, will both compete!' 'The final count is One hundred and Fourteen!' The news would then spread outward in furtive discussions until it reached everyone in the grounds.

Draupadi heard the whispers of the villagers as her doli passed. She saw women with uncovered heads sit next to their men on the grass. They looked openly, enviously at her jewels sparkling as they caught the sun through the sheer curtains. Did they wish they were in her place? Did she wish she was in theirs? They were almost at the entrance of the amphitheatre. How much smaller it had seemed from the windows of the women's palace! The sweet smell of black aloe emanating from it, was overpowering. Draupadi drew a deep breath as the nausea returned to her belly.

✳

The head priest, stationed next to the blazing sacred fire on the side, stood up and blew his conch towards the sky, creating a deafening, haunting sound that seemed to reverberate miles. The kettle drums started up again, drowning out the cheers of the seated crowd as the various names of Princess Draupadi of Panchala were announced in the amphitheatre. King Drupada, dressed in a white silken dhoti and shoulder scarf with his huge triangular golden crown atop his head and gold jewels adorning his body, stopped his conversation with Krishna and looked at the royal entrance. Draupadi's twin brother Prince Dhrishtadyumna, similarly attired, stood up and walked to receive his sister.

Among the audience, there was an expectant commotion. Sixteen days of celebration had lead up to this one moment. Their eyes all trained on the royal entrance as Draupadi's entourage filtered in and moved towards the royal women's enclosure on one side. Unlike the others, this one was entirely fenced off by high, painted wooden planks and shielded in front by almost invisible curtains. It afforded a perfect view, not only of the goings-on in the circular arena, but of the hundred other royal corrals dispersed high and low across the amphitheatre. Next to it was a gilded platform with King Drupada's gold-plated silver throne and two smaller thrones, one for Dhrishtadyumna and the other for the guest of honour, Krishna. In between the corrals, around the arena, were wooden seats for hundreds of noblemen, priests and rich merchants, each fenced off from the other with a separate entry.

In the earthen centrestage was a wooden crane, forty feet high. Suspended from its revolving tentacle at the very top, a stuffed fish with a large eye stared and swayed. At the toe of this machine was a wide, sunken metal plate filled with water and, some distance away, resting on a table, lay a bow almost the size of a man, its thick string left unstrung next to it. Five arrows made to fit this giant bow stood in a neat line against the table.

A hush fell over the stadium as Draupadi entered. In the silence, the tinkle of her anklets could be heard even in the higher rows. Tiny gasps and murmurs were heard in the gathering, as each man, and king, stole a glance at her.

Draupadi heard the gasping as she walked. She looked around from the corner of her eye. Sitting in royal corrals all over the amphitheatre, were kings from across the land. They were dressed in full regalia, silken dhotis and scarves, golden earrings, necklaces, armbands, wristbands, belts and anklets. Each wore an inherited crown with his royal insignia and precious gems. They lounged on cushioned half-beds, their swords, bows and maces resting on woven carpets. Some were muscular, others corpulent. Some carried moustaches, yet others were shaven. Some were surrounded by relatives and lackeys, some sat together, others were solitary. All were looking at her. She felt like covering her face with her arms and bolting to the privacy of her chambers. This was no ordinary scrutiny. This was unlike the gaping of the guards and the deferential curiosity of the villagers. She knew that a little over a hundred men looking at her at this moment wanted to own her.

She reached her brother, who took her by the arm to escort her to the women's enclosure. She glanced up at his prim face and read nothing. Her twin was too taken in by decorum and ceremony to show any support or feeling.

She passed her father's podium and surreptitiously looked at his grey, wisened frame. He seemed to be looking at her indulgently, but upon trying to catch his eye, she realised he was looking just above her head into nothing. An old disappointment threatened to take over just as she caught a familiar eye. Sitting next to her father was Krishna, a man well past his adolescent days, he was black as night, his handsome face almost cherubic, his brilliant black eyes shining with perpetual mischief. Widely acknowledged as the most powerful of all the warrior kings, Krishna was dressed in simple but elegant robes and the trademark peacock feather in his crown. He was smiling fondly at her. In his hand he held a pink, blooming lotus flower and, as she passed him, he held it up to his nose. Draupadi was torn between despair and anger at his teasing behaviour. Anger and pride won as she extended her chin out and looked away. Krishna's smile broadened mischievously behind the flower.

Dhrishtadyumna took his sister to her enclosure, where she sat on a cushioned day-bed with Neela and the other maidens at her feet. He turned around and addressed the stadium loudly, 'Welcome, Kings and Princes to this *Swayamwara*. My father and I are glad to be your humble hosts on this occasion. Each of you is endowed with impeccable birth, lineage and accomplishments. Still, it will take a man of considerable strength, agility and talent to complete the task I am about to put before you.' He pointed to the revolving crane in the arena, 'The eye of the moving fish is the target. There is the bow. String it and pierce the target with one of five arrows. There is but one condition. You cannot look at the target as you aim. The water must be your eye-glass.'

A buzz arose among the kings in response to this unexpected condition, their faces sceptical. The rest of the audience seemed elated. Aha, was the look on their faces, now it would get interesting.

Dhrishtadyumna continued, 'My sister, Draupadi, will choose her husband from those of you who succeed at this great feat.'

He turned to face Draupadi and said in the same voice, 'I will now recite to you, Sister, the names of those who have come to compete for your hand. Duryodhana, Durvisaha, Durmukha and Dushpradharshana, Vivinsati, Vikarna, Saha . . .'

Draupadi knew the names even though she recognised no faces. Determined not to look at Krishna again, she looked around the audience. The noblemen with their gilded turbans sat in the left wing of the stadium. The favourites were at the feet of royals in the enclosures.

'. . . Dushasana, Yuyutsu, Vayuvega and Bhimsenavegarava. Ugrayudha, Valaki, Kanakayu, and Virochana . . .'

The priests sat together in the right wing, a sea of shaved heads, loose flesh and plain dhotis. Some were praying, others talking softly among themselves and some . . . Draupadi's eyes suddenly stopped wandering.

Sitting in the midst of the priest's enclosure was the most un-priestly man she had ever seen. He wore his head shaved, a plain dhoti and the customary sacred string around his chest like the others, but he was distinctly uncommon. In the prime of youth, his craggy, handsome face had an air of the regal and his body was broad and tightened. He was sitting but she knew he was very tall. He looked around with an expression of ease but held himself like a stretched catapult. As he heard Dhrishtadyumna recite each of the names, he looked up at the corrals with recognition and . . . suspicion? He seemed to slink further and further into the human mass in which he sat, trying, it seemed, to blend in . . . almost even, to hide.

'. . . Sakuni, Sauvala, Vrisaka, and Vrihadvala . . .'

Draupadi couldn't take her eyes off the priest. His shoulder cloth had shifted for a moment and she was sure she saw tell-tale archer's scars, left by the bow, on his skin. Suddenly, he looked right at her and she started and looked away as if caught doing something forbidden. Almost immediately, she felt ridiculous. She was a royal and could look where she liked! Still, her heart didn't stop racing until he looked away. Then, she stole one last glimpse.

'. . . Vrihadratha, Valhika, Sisupala and Jarasandha. These kings have come from far and wide for you, Sister. Choose your Lord from those who complete the task. I now invite the first contender to begin the *Swayamwara*.' Dhrishtadyumna turned and walked to his throne. The priests in the fire-pit resumed their chanting and a small group of musicians, seated near the royal entrance, began playing their instruments. There was a low buzz in the audience.

Draupadi looked at Neela, who gazed at her with a worried brow. She shook her head and said softly, 'I'm alright.' She looked covertly at Krishna, serenely smiling to himself as he sat next to her father, and sighed. They said every pubescent girl and even most grown-up women fancied themselves in love with him. He had many wives, she knew, but had always thought she was special. Never had a visit ended without a magnificent bouquet of pink lotus flowers being sent to her chambers. Never had he failed to smile and wave up at her when she had peeked out of the windows to see him departing. Had she just read too much into overtures of friendship? Her bruised heart refused to believe.

There came cheering from around a corral as one of the kings made his way down to the arena. He was large and barrel-shaped, with bulky arms and thighs. He tweaked his black moustache and thumped his arms as he climbed down stairs, egged on by his friends.

'Who is he?' Draupadi asked Neela.

After a quick consultation with Saumya, Neela answered, 'Duryodhana, the bull.'

Draupadi bit her lip. Duryodhana was called the bull because of his immense strength and style of battle, in which he charged his enemy with a lowered head. He was believed to be one of the most likely to complete this task. He was also believed to be callous and manipulative, accused in some circles of murdering his cousins to usurp their kingdom.

Duryodhana approached the giant bow and tried to lift it with his right hand. He failed. His stance faltered as he grasped it with both hands and heaved it into a standing position. He tried to bend the bow and string it. He failed, again and again. Using all his might, he bent the bow one last time, but the string slipped from his large fingers and the giant bow sprung back with a loud twang. Duryodhana was thrown to the ground and his crown fell off his head.

Many laughed but most didn't dare. Duryodhana looked like thunder as he stormed out of the amphitheatre. Draupadi glanced at the strange priest, who was laughing at the dusty Duryodhana. His face looked softer when he laughed, his chest and shoulders undulating with movement. Draupadi couldn't help a slight smile. Then, she remembered her previous despair and very quickly looked away.

One by one, the kings came down into the arena. Warriors were they, each one confident of taking the prize. They slapped their arms and thighs, tweaked their hair and some even addressed the gathering before they attempted the feat. They all returned shoulders slumped, unsuccessful.

One king, whom Saumya believed was Sisupala, king of the Chedis, faced Draupadi from the arena and proclaimed, 'Draupadi shall be mine!' This launched the maidens into undignified fits of giggles, which were augmented when he returned to his chair, unable even to lift the bow.

Another king, Sunama, spent such an inordinate amount of time studying the bow, arrows and structure that the audience began to heckle him. He cast a vexed glance around and attempted to string the bow while it laid horizontal, stamping one end with his feet and trying to bend the other with his hands. Though innovative, this comical strategy didn't work and many in the unforgiving audience loudly told him not to embarrass his clan. This infuriated Sunama's brother, Suvarcha, and he stomped down to the arena and ordered his flustered brother back to their corral. He then attempted to lift the bow with an angry jerk and discovered, too late, that his brother's endeavours had buried the foot of the bow into the dust, a handful of which was tossed into his face unceremoniously. Furious, he marched out of the arena.

As the morning passed into midday, Draupadi grew tired of the spectacle. Only one king, an elephant of a man, had managed to string the bow so far, applauded generously by the audience. However, his archery skills had left much to be desired and he returned after shooting the arrow into the white canopy above. The sun's heat too seemed to pierce the unfortunate cloth, rendering everyone lethargic. Even the musicians yawned as they played.

The kings were less confident now as they descended to face their nemesis. An attempt had to be made for fear of losing face, but no longer did they strut or demonstrate their strength. Each bested by the bow, walked back to his corral, silently blaming king Drupada for creating such an impossible task. Back in their enclosures, they tossed their heads and sneered that, at this rate, Draupadi would remain a virgin forever.

Draupadi now looked at the contenders with disdain, expecting them to fail even before their attempts. She remembered what Krishna had said; no ordinary man, not even a king, could be her husband. It seemed that this stadium was full of ordinary men. Forgetting, for the moment, the gloom that thinking of Krishna usually sent her into, she glanced again at the priest. This time, he was leaning back and looking at the present contender with a look of derision. As the contender walked away, he turned to his neighbour and made an obviously sarcastic comment, slapping his own arm in the process. Anger rushed through Draupadi. What right did he have to sit there and jeer at the kings, who were, at least, trying? If he be so confident of his own ability, why didn't he undertake the task himself? After all, there is no rule against a priest trying for the hand of a princess! Her chin went up just as he turned to look at her. Their eyes met for the first time. Draupadi, who had begun to perceive, from looking upon him so often, that she was acquainted with this priest who behaved with the arrogance of a warrior, frowned at him. The priest's eyes were questioning at first and then, he looked away, carelessly dismissing her gaze.

Draupadi opened her mouth and then closed it. How dare that lowly priest insult a royal princess! Was not looking at her an insult? Never mind. How dare he? She felt like a caged tigress. She wanted to go over there and ... and ... hit him! No, not hit him, but make him ... what? Look at her again? Yes ... no ... oh, she didn't know. She glared at his face.

Suddenly, there was a roar from the audience, as cheering and booing erupted in chorus. Draupadi turned her glare to the arena. A rough-looking man, his muscular body dressed in royal robes had picked up the bow and was in the process of stringing it quite competently.

She leaned towards Neela, still looking at the man, 'Who is he?'

Neela replied, 'Karna, the famed archer. Duryodhana's adopted brother.'

'What? The charioteer's son?' Draupadi couldn't believe it.

At the centre, Karna had finished stringing the giant bow with some effort and was fixing an arrow into it, his eyes downward on the reflection of the target in the metal plate. The audience, priests and musicians went silent.

Neela whispered, 'Yes. That's why some were booing him.'

Draupadi had had enough insolence for one day. She said loudly, 'And does he presume I will marry the son of a servant?'

Neela gasped. Karna had been pulling the bowstring back, his aim sure and steady. He stopped. Very few hadn't heard Draupadi's remark. He lowered the bow slowly and looked at Draupadi, menacing resentment on his weathered, young face. Then he deftly unstrung the bow, threw it to the ground and strode out of the amphitheatre.

King Drupada and Dhrishtadyumna turned and stared at Draupadi with barely suppressed anger. She had insulted not only Karna, but the entire Kuru clan, who had adopted him as their own. Affronts like these led to ill-conceived wars among their kind. Draupadi turned to Krishna, unwittingly seeking his support, but he continued, smiling absently, to look into the distance. She returned the gaze of her father and brother with brave defiance, even as uncertainty flooded her resolution.

The assembled kings were now united in their dissatisfaction. Had no one been able to attempt the task, the royals may have argued that it was impossible. But the mighty archer Karna had almost finished it, leaving the rest with flushed faces and injured prides.

The audience was, once again, alert and talkative. The priests and musicians had resumed their ministrations, yet the atmosphere of festivity had disappeared. Irate murmurs filled the corrals. There were a few more contenders but none came forward. Draupadi had openly rejected the one man who might have been her husband.

King Drupada sat rigid in his throne. For him to address the gathering now would be to openly acknowledge Draupadi's lapse and swallow his pride. However, if no more kings came forth to compete, he would have to call off the *Swayamwara* and declare his daughter a maiden for life. Next to him, Krishna hummed softly to himself, his eyes casually scanning the priest's wing of the amphitheatre. He had been the one to suggest this task, with its extreme difficulty, to Drupada. Now, it seemed that Krishna had either had a lapse in judgement or an ulterior motive.

Draupadi felt strangely numb, despite being faced with Krishna's rejection, her family's wrath and the prospect of life-long maidenhood. Next to her, Neela had begun praying softly. Her eyes wandered back to the priest's wing. He was looking at her. This time he held her gaze, his expression an enigma. His eyes were no longer laughing or derisive or questioning. They were hard, set in rock. Draupadi's heart began to race again. As eternal moments passed, he seemed to be trying to see within her, weighing her, challenging her. Then, still looking at her, he got up.

The audience was aroused, the kings amused and the priests outraged. Who did this young stripling think he was? 'Sit down!' they shouted, to no avail. The tall, young priest strode to the centre of the stadium, ignoring their calls. Foolishness, utter foolishness, the older audience members muttered among themselves. How could a priest, who would have spent his entire life studying the sacred texts, even hope to compete with warrior kings who had been trained in physical combat since birth? This young man walked like a tiger in heat, his eyes fixed on the princess. They were convinced he would regret this childish daring in a few moments.

Draupadi sat, transfixed, as the young priest reached the arena and circled the bow and crane twice, studying them carefully. She should discourage him like she did Karna, but her mind couldn't find her voice. Then, she watched, astonished, as he turned and walked towards King Drupada's platform. Upon reaching it, the priest ignored the others and saluted Krishna respectfully by folding his hands and bowing low.

Draupadi noticed as Krishna smiled affectionately and nodded his head at the priest. She was sure they knew each other well, even though there was no outward demonstration of acquaintance from either.

Then, the priest turned and walked back to the bow. Draupadi, in fact, the entire audience gasped collectively as he lifted it heavily into a standing position and bent the bow with a grunt. His nimble fingers quickly strung the giant, and he tugged at the string to test it. He picked up an arrow and walked towards the crane.

Utter silence once again arrested the stadium. Draupadi held her breath in anticipation, as her hand involuntarily stole to Neela's, gripping it tightly.

The priest took aim, his eyes set downward on the reflection, following the fish's eye in the watery, metal plate. He pulled back the bowstring, slow and deliberate, then fired the arrow with a loud twang.

For a moment Draupadi couldn't tell if the screeching arrow had found its mark. In that infinitesimal, yet infinite moment, every eye in the stadium searched, waited, desperately for the outcome. Then, from forty feet in the air, the target fell to the ground and, in the dust, lay a stuffed fish, its eye neatly pierced by the shaft of an arrow.

The uproar was like a thousand elephants in battle. People stood up from their seats to get a better look. The priests' enclosure erupted in applause and furtive discussion. The maidens screeched in excitement. Only the kings sat silent, speechless. In the arena, the tall priest picked up the target and held it high over his head, so all could see. Then, he walked to King Drupada's platform and laid the target at the king's feet, his eyes never once straying to witness Draupadi's reaction.

Her reaction was as violent inside, as it was restrained outside. For the first time in her life, she felt dumbfounded, powerless and out of control. She looked at Neela and saw a mirror of her own emotions. Not a king, not even a nobleman, this priest, whoever he was, had done what the most powerful men in the land could not. He had just won her hand in marriage!

King Drupada stood and picked up the target, inspecting it thoroughly with a controlled look on his face. The priest stood silently in front of the platform, amidst the deafening clamour that filled the amphitheatre and, by now, the entire palace grounds.

The king showed the target to a grinning Krishna and they talked in muted tones. The king was momentarily agitated at something Krishna said, but then regained his composure and bowed his head in compliance. Drupada walked to the edge of the platform and said in a booming voice, 'Hear me now.'

The din quieted to expectancy. Everybody wanted to know what would happen now.

Drupada continued, 'Is there any other man, royal, noble or priest, who would like to attempt the task?'

Nothing but a quiet audience answered him. Nobody, especially a king, wanted to follow this performance.

King Drupada waited for a few moments and then said, 'If there are no more contenders, then this Swayamwara has come to an end. My daughter is now this man's bride.'

Draupadi didn't hear the eruption in the stadium and beyond. She didn't hear Neela crying next to her. Words echoed in her mind over and over. 'My daughter is now this man's bride.' 'No ordinary man, not even a king, can be your husband.' 'Draupadi shall be mine!' 'You should never be perfect ...' 'My daughter is now this man's bride ...'

Unseen hands put the golden platter back into her hands. Unseen hands grasped her arms and led her to the centre of the arena to face him. There he stood, looking at her walk towards him. The oil and incense, burning in the plate she carried, blew into her face as she halted, facing him. Forgotten were the hundreds around her, under whose gaze she had previously shrunk. Forgotten was her despair, her defiance along with her righteous indignation, as she looked upon his person.

His eyes were the colour of wet earth, his eyebrows almost meeting at the centre of his forehead. The skin on his rugged looking face was actually quite smooth and tanned and his lips were a restrained version of hers. His chin was like hers too, strong, but wider ... stronger. The curly hair on his chest, shoulders and arms, veiled faint scars from what could only be combat. His hands and feet seemed almost royal, as if they regularly met with cleaning tools and the softening sandalwood paste.

She met his gaze. He seemed to challenge her to refuse him. She looked down into her platter. The ochre, rice and sacred water waited patiently for her to realise her inevitable future, her destiny. They brooked no argument and, in that infinitesimal moment, she had none to give them. When she looked up, it was with acceptance. His eyes softened and she felt something spark within her. Was it love? No, it was awareness. Of him, this stranger. Her husband.

BHISHMA'S ADMISSION

❦

'$\mathcal{I}$ didn't want to kill you.'

Arjuna, Prince of Indraprastha, bent like a child over the old man's body, his rough, grimy hands pressed against his mouth and nose as if they could somehow stem the tears streaming from his swollen eyes. He rocked back and forth ever so slightly, 'Granduncle Bhishma, please ... please,' his voice broke, his soft weeping renewed as a fresh wave of guilt, horror and disbelief washed over him.

The old man's face remained unmoving, save a few disobedient strands of his flowing, silver beard that danced to the chilly evening breeze. His thin braid of grey hair, liberated by the absence of the royal crown, intertwined with one of the heavy gold loops that always hung from his earlobes, as if to protect it from unwanted attention. The visible front of his body, dressed in a soiled white tunic and guarded by an intricately carved, gold-plated armour, looked as if in deep slumber. A cruelly deceptive slumber, for in contrast was his naked back, embedded with five deadly arrowheads, pressed against the bloody, blackened mud of the Kurukshetra battlefield.

Indistinguishable was the great Bhishma of Hastinapur's royal blood amidst the million streams of dirty red, common liquid that flowed for miles around him, over undulating hills and the bodies of thousands of fallen soldiers. The colours that painted the battlefield reflected the chilling aftermath of the day's slaughter, brown dirt and scarlet blood brutally raped virgin white cloth, nauseating pink and dark grey organs seeped out of tattered wheat flesh, burnt wood and blackened metal, tainted gold jewels peeping out of unsacred earth. The only purity lay in the somber orange setting sun in masculine blue twilight, and the weeping witnesses, the desperate brothers and fathers that searched for brothers and sons lost in mounds of human mass, the good doctors who mercifully murdered the few that remained suspended between life and death and the mini-armies of undertakers that cleared the ground for fresh carnage tomorrow. The night would once again be illuminated by two giant bonfires, one on either side of the battlefield. The last light of the dead.

But no one touched Bhishma's body. No one dared.

Earlier, many a doctor had scrambled to him as he lay on the ground, freshly stricken, Arjuna's thick arrows protruding from his back. The legendary Bhishma's fall had brought the day's fighting to an abrupt end, as both sides remained suspended in indecision. The battlefield had been silent save soft murmurs, the occasional clank of armour and the nervous exclamations of the horses and elephants.

Bhishma, in agony, had calmly instructed the doctors to break the arrows so that he may rest on his back and move him to an elevated side of the battlefield. Once laid on the ground next to a stream, he had refused treatment. The only concession he allowed was a small cushion under his head.

His royal comrades and relatives had hovered around him. He was, after all, the commander of their army. He gave them his last command; 'No one,' he said, was to move him, dead or alive, until the last day's battle was finished and this war was over once and for all. He then closed his eyes and closed, they remained. His grandnephews, the Kauravas, led by Prince Duryodhana, whispered furtively among themselves even as they sent word for the army to retreat and stood near him to pay their last respects. For them, their indestructible Commander-in-chief was already a dead man and a replacement needed to be appointed immediately for the sake of victory. Eventually, as dusk approached, even the most faithful left and returned to the Kaurava camp. The battle still needed to be fought tomorrow, albeit at a respectable distance from Bhishma's body.

' . . . forgive me . . . please.'

Prince Arjuna tenderly, instinctively reached out to touch Bhishma's hand and then pulled back abruptly. His breath came out in an angry rasp, in disgust at his insolence. He barely remembered the moments after his arrows had pierced his Granduncle's back. He had been pulled away by his brother-in-law and charioteer, Krishna, even as every inch of him screamed to go to Bhishma and undo what he had just done. Krishna had commanded their soldiers to retreat back to the Pandava army camp as the Kaurava army stood shuffling helplessly without their commander. Back at their camp, Arjuna was surrounded noisily by his brothers, Yudhishthira, Bhimsena, Nakula and Sahadeva, his mother Kunti and his wife Draupadi. He had kept quiet as they had all debated with Krishna the point of fighting one's own family for the sake of a kingdom. Krishna had consoled them, had reassured them of the righteousness of their actions and they retired to their tents, one by one, free from the crushing burden that was Arjuna's to carry. It had been his arrows, shot from his shoulder. He would never be free. He had waited till the candles in the tents flickered into the darkness and crept back to the battlefield.

He looked down at Bhishma's still face, his bloodied clothes, his lifeless limbs, 'How can I ask your forgiveness when I will never be able to forgive myself,' he whispered and buried his face in his hands once more.

'Nonsense. There is . . . nothing to forgive . . . now bring me some water.'

Arjuna's eyes flew open. Bhishma was looking at him tenderly, his parched lips quivering with the effort of speech, '. . . water.'

Arjun scrambled to his feet and ran towards the stream, barely able to see through his tears. He scooped up water in his palms and held them over Bhishma's mouth so that he could drink.

A few drops were all Bhishma allowed himself. Enough to speak.

Bhishma took a deep breath and winced with the effort. He continued in a raspy, struggling whisper, 'I feel no pain . . .'

Fresh tears tumbled out of Arjuna's eyes.

Bhishma, who had seen a thousand men die pitifully before his eyes, could not bear to see his grandnephew cry. 'My child. Stop weeping. I feel no pain. My body is already dead and can hurt me no more.'

Arjuna was overcome. 'Your body is dead because of me. Those are my arrows in your back. It is my fault. Had I not listened to Krishna and disallowed Shikandi from standing in my chariot, had I stopped this . . . this madness in time, we would never have had war. Granduncle Bhishma, I don't care about the kingdom, I don't care about glory or riches. It is worthless if I have to murder my own blood, my family . . .'

'Stop,' Bhishma paused for a moment in thought. 'Shikandi,' he whispered, 'I knew her a long time ago. She called herself Amba then . . .' He blinked and looked at Arjuna, 'Listen to me, Arjuna. You did what you had to do. Krishna was right.

By having Shikandi, a woman, stand in your chariot, you were able to divert me long enough to fire your arrows. I could not have fired at a woman, especially not that one.' He looked away, let out a slow sigh and said softly, almost to himself, 'In fact, Krishna has been right in more ways than that ...'

His eyes turned to Arjuna once more and smiled, 'The body is a deceptive thing. I am quite happy to be free of it, for my mind is finally ... clear.' He paused to catch his breath, 'Over the last few hours, as my limbs went numb, I have felt a release ... bliss like never before. I feel ... like a man released from a lifetime in prison.'

'It is you who have given me the greatest gift of all ... clarity. And for that, I must thank you, my child ...'

Arjuna looked down at Bhishma's lifeless hands, the large but gentle hands that had tweaked his chin as a toddler, had carefully guided him in holding a bow for the first time as a child and had firmly rested on his shoulder to give moral support as an adult. He took one and cradled it carefully in his own. He said nothing.

Bhishma felt none of the warmth in Arjuna's hands. He did feel the anguish in Arjuna's heart. He looked at Arjuna's bowed head, 'You know Arjuna, all my life I tried ... to live by the rules of Dharma.' He chuckled softly in his throat, 'And I did ... till the very end. Do you know what good has come of it?' He raised an eyebrow at Arjuna.

Arjuna found his voice with difficulty, 'No.'

'None. My life has been a complete waste. I realise that now ... ,' Bhishma continued to smile.

Arjuna shook his head violently, 'No. Don't say that, Granduncle Bhishma. You are a hero. You have been an example, not only for me but for all of us, my brothers and cousins ...'

Bhishma's eyes looked away angrily, 'Your cousins, the Kauravas, learnt nothing of Dharma. They learned lowly greed and lust,' he breathed heavily, 'Like thieves . . . they stole your kingdom, your rightful inheritance from you and your brothers. You are right in fighting them.'

Arjuna's fervent eyes shouted but his words did not come easily, 'If you felt this way, then why did you command their army, Granduncle? Why did you not come to our side?'

Bhishma smiled the sad smile of hindsight. 'I had a very good reason at that time, my Arjuna. It had to do with dharma . . . how little I have understood of that elusive concept. How much I have to atone for,' he paused to gasp for air, 'I will tell you the reason I fought on the side of greed and faithlessness against the virtuous and blameless. But first, . . . some more water please.'

Bhishma drank more water from Arjuna's fingers this time. Then, he looked up at the night and began to talk, 'I fought with the Kauravas because I had pledged allegiance to the throne of Hastinapur when my father was King and I, the crown prince. . . . Allegiance to the throne, regardless of who sat on it. It was my vow, and to keep it, my Dharma,' he paused for a moment, 'Dharma . . . To tell the truth, to be fair . . . to be virtuous, to have morals, to gather religious and spiritual merit, to fear sin, to act righteously.' He took a breath, 'It is what they teach us as children. Truth. Such a simple word. What is truth?'

Arjuna was quiet. It was a rhetorical question, addressed to the stars in the distance.

'I have never told a lie, Arjuna. Not even when a small lie could have done a world of good . . . Is that truth?'

Bhishma continued slowly, brokenly, 'When I was crown prince of Hastinapur, my father Santanu, your great-grandfather, fell in love with a fisherwoman. She refused to marry him unless he guaranteed that her children would inherit the throne. To assist the marriage, I vowed that I would renounce the throne and never marry or have children. I vowed to live a celibate life. I kept that vow, Arjuna. Even when my stepmother, having lost both her sons, begged me to ascend to the throne and have children for the sake of the people, I kept my vow. Do you know what I told her? I said that I would give up not only the kingdom but the world of the Gods, I would let the sun go dark, let the world end but I would never give up the truth. I refused to let my uttering of that vow be a lie.'

'That one decision changed the fate of the entire kingdom. My desperate stepmother then asked her illegitimate son, a hermit named Vyasa, to impregnate her son's wives. They were petrified of him, of his dirty, rough appearance and the children of that union bore the signs of their rape. Your father was a weak, sickly man till he died and your Uncle Dhritarashtra, the King of Hastinapur, is not only blind but is also of weak character. His sons have inherited the worst of him.'

Bhishma looked at Arjuna and said in small voice, 'I could have been King of Hastinapur, a just king. I could have ensured the kingdom went into capable hands after me. I . . . I could have been your grandfather.'

Arjuna's voice was choked, 'You have been no less than a grandfather.'

Bhishma looked away, 'Does a grandfather allow his grandson's wife to be stripped in a public court, before his very eyes?'

Arjuna closed his eyes and tried desperately, as he had done countless times before, to block from his mind's eye the vision of his wife Draupadi as she was on that unholy day. He failed once again as his memory replayed, fresh as if it were moments ago, Draupadi's small frame huddled on the floor, taut hands clutching an ineffective cloth to her naked breasts, under the scrutiny of every man in court. He saw vividly her loose flowing hair sweep the slabs of stone beneath her dainty feet, the stain of womanhood on her flimsy shift, the tears that shrouded her face and neck, the anger, disgust and horror in her eyes as she looked at him watching helplessly. . . . Arjuna's eyes flew open, a familiar rage engulfing every particle of his body, every fragment of his being. He wanted to destroy his cousins Duryodhana and Dushasana for what they did to Draupadi that day.

It had started as a friendly game of dice between cousins. A few lost rounds and Arjuna and his brothers were slaves, bet away by elder brother Yudhishthira, along with their wives and kingdom of Indraprastha, in a game against Duryodhana. A mere sport of chance, an amusement to pass the hours ended in his cousin Dushasana dragging Draupadi into open court and attempting to strip her, even as the elders and courtiers looked at their feet in mortification.

'I was sitting right there, Arjuna,' Bhishma whispered, 'She looked at me and pleaded, begged me to save her modesty, her honour, to command Dushasana to stop. Do you recall what I said? I told her that since she was technically now a slave and belonged to Duryodhana, he was justified by law to do as he pleased with her. A daughter in my own family . . . an innocent girl . . . the shame . . .' Bhishma's face remained stoic, belying the storm in his eyes.

Arjuna couldn't look at him. He turned towards the battlefield that reeked of devastation. To him, this war was as much about avenging the insult to Draupadi's honour as it was about regaining a rightful kingdom. Only Krishna, his dear Krishna, had come to Draupadi's rescue that day and stopped Dushasana before he could completely disrobe her. An act that had shamed the blind King into restoring the losses of the game back to Arjuna and his brothers. Of course, no sooner than they had walked away, they were summoned back into court, challenged to another round by Duryodhana. This time, the stakes were different; the losing party was to go on a thirteen-year exile into the forest, forsaking the crown and the kingdom.

Arjuna looked at Bhishma's face, noticing how he had aged since the last time they talked, thirteen years ago. Never could he have imagined that their reunion would be like this.

Bhishma sighed, 'I'm sorry Arjuna. I failed Draupadi. I failed all of you,' he looked at Arjuna's face, 'Will you forgive this old man on his deathbed?'

Arjuna's heart flailed, caught between blind anger over his wife's mistreatment and love for his Granduncle. He could not help but think that one word from Bhishma would have silenced all that day. One word would have prevented a thirteen-year exile, prevented this war. One word and Bhishma would have escaped this death.

Arjuna massaged his forehead to clear it. What was the point of hindsight, of railing against cruel fate? It would not, could not bring back those thirteen lost years or the thousands dead before him on the battlefield. He did the right thing, 'Like you said to me a few moments ago, Granduncle, there is nothing to forgive. You followed the rules of Dharma . . . the gods will welcome you into their abode.'

'I hope the gods know better,' Bhishma managed softly, 'I hope they will send me back to try again, to be a better man than I have been in this life,' he looked at Arjuna, 'I take solace in the fact that Krishna has been there for you in my absence. He has broken all the rules of Dharma in his short life, yet only good has come of it.'

'I know he was the one who instructed you to put these arrows in my back. You may feel anger towards him for that, but the truth is, had you not struck me, I would have likely destroyed much of your army and ensured your defeat. Now, there is a greater chance your side will win this war. You need not feel any guilt, Arjuna. You are fighting for a greater good ... you will establish a virtuous throne in Hastinapur and Indraprastha. You will give a better life to the countless subjects that live in the kingdom ... no, listen to me ...'

Arjuna held back his words.

Bhishma continued, conviction lending strength to his voice, 'As a warrior, this is the most honourable way to die, on a battlefield against another of equal skill. I have lived my life Arjuna, a long, unnatural life without feeling ... without love,' his eyes glazed over, 'For a long time I have been like a chariot rolling down a hill without a horse to give it direction or a passenger to give it purpose. I am ready for death ... in fact, I welcome it.'

He looked into Arjuna's eyes, 'Win this war, Arjuna, for my sake. Establish a new Dharma, one that looks towards a higher truth. And live a good life, my child. Live like I never did ... that is the blessing I give you.'

Arjuna's heart wrenched. There was nothing more to be said, except, 'I will.'

Bhishma smiled a tender smile that Arjuna would remember for the rest of his days. And then, he closed his eyes, 'Now leave ...'

Twilight had long passed, giving way to black, starry skies. Giant bonfires raged in the distance, shooting flickering sparks, like fireflies, into the night. The smell of incinerating oil and wood slowly replaced the lingering hum of death. For what seemed like eternity sat Arjuna next to Bhishma's silent body.

DURYODHANA'S DECISION

❧

It was an ocean of gold and he was floating in it. Golden water, golden waves and golden fish that bobbed their ruby eyes over the surface to smile and greet him. He dived and splashed like a child in its shimmery warmth, giggling with glee. Suddenly, a silver fish-monster appeared out of nowhere and grabbed his shoulder with its jagged metal jaws, shaking him furiously. . . .

Duryodhana, Prince of Hastinapur, jerked awake. His sweat-laden temples and heaving chest were witnessed apprehensively by the man who stood above him in the large palace hall, lightly shaking his shoulder.

Duryodhana leaped off the stool on which he had dozed, almost knocking the other man off his own feet. He tried valiantly to appear alert and in control as he fumbled with his royal robes and exclaimed in a hoarse, loud voice that echoed in the vast chamber, 'Oh noble king, forgive me. I was in deep meditation over an important matter.'

The man, an elderly king from the north-eastern regions, looked at the prince before him with amused eyes. Duryodhana's massive, bulky frame swayed comically from having jumped up too quickly and his crown was perched dangerously on one side of his large, dishevelled head. The black, thick hairs on his neck, shoulders, arms, chest and navel stood on end like those of an angry dog and his large mustache, usually oiled and aimed dramatically at the heavens, had become quite unkempt.

Despite this, the king bowed his head and replied politely, 'Of course, your highness. You must have many important matters on your mind. After all, it is no small task you have been given by King Yudhishthira of Indraprastha. Or, should I say, Emperor Yudhishthira, after yesterday's events.'

A green vein on Duryodhana's neck twitched sharply at the mention of the word 'emperor' but his toothy smile gave away none of his thoughts, 'Yes, Rajasuya sacrifices are rare, so I suppose he deserves that honour. It is quite a feat to be a king without enemies these days.' Duryodhana rubbed his neck.

The king replied, 'Yes, virtually impossible in most parts. Is that the only requirement of a king who wishes to perform the Rajasuya and declare himself an emperor?'

That word again. Duryodhana shuffled his feet uncomfortably, 'It is one of the requirements. The king in question must follow Dharma, have happy subjects, powerful allies and a significant amount of wealth to bear the expense of the sacrifice itself.'

The elderly king nodded enthusiastically, 'Oh yes, yes. If what I have witnessed this past week is anything to go by, Yudhishthira is truly blessed with all of that. He seems like the epitome of Dharma and his subjects obviously worship him. With allies like the mighty Krishna and the seemingly infinite wealth of Indraprastha that he has so generously shared with all of us during our very comfortable stay here, he is, the most deserving . . .'

Duryodhana yawned loudly and interrupted, 'Yes, yes . . . most deserving. Now, did you perhaps want to see *me* about something, oh noble king?'

The old king's eyes widened a little at this obvious discourtesy, but his own politeness didn't fail him, 'I did. I have taken my leave of King, excuse me, Emperor Yudhishthira, Krishna and the elders in the palace. Before I leave, however, I would like to present, to Yudhishthira, a token of my allegiance and friendship. I have been informed that you are receiving gifts on his behalf for the period of the sacrifice. May I entrust you with my gift?'

A tiny muscle in Duryodhana's left eye seemed to have taken on a life of its own while the King spoke. He rubbed it irritably, 'You may, o' King. My cousin Yudhishthira has indeed, put me in charge of receiving gifts on his behalf this week,' he shrugged carelessly towards the huge, palatial hall behind him, laden with countless precious gifts that were stacked as high as the ceiling. Jewels lay strewn over crumpled cloths of the finest brocade and silk from even the most distant of kingdoms. Hundreds of figurines of animals carved in precious stones, intricate paintings on marble and crystal, murals made from gems the size of rocks all leaned on one another in disarray. 'What is it you wish to leave for him?'

The king threw a dubious glance at the chaotic hall behind Duryodhana, turned and began to slowly proceed towards the door that led into the sun-lit courtyard, 'It is outside.'

Duryodhana followed suit. He squinted as the massive doors were opened for them by the palace guards. Not only because of the afternoon sun, which was indeed imposingly bright, but because of the golden vision that stood before him. Intricately carved, studded with countless, shimmery sea pearls, shaded by white, silken umbrellas and pulled by four glorious, virgin-white steeds of the finest blood, was a chariot of gold. Duryodhana blinked, 'Is that ... ?'

The king confirmed the thought proudly, 'Solid gold.'

Duryodhana walked around the chariot and ran his fingers across the blunt peaks and valleys of its surface. His fingers then reached the horses. He stroked their backs and shoulders, feeling the strength and perfection of thoroughbred bone and muscle. For a moment, Duryodhana had a vision of himself driving that chariot across an open field and letting the horses break into a battle run. Then, he remembered. The chariot was not to be his, but belonged to his cousins. Just like everything else.

The palace guards and footmen watched him with lowered but careful eyes. Duryodhana had felt their gaze all throughout the week and knew they had an account of everything that passed into his hands. He forced his features into a smile, 'I'm sure, cousin Yudhishthira and his brothers would be very pleased with your gift, o' king. You may leave it in my care and I shall personally see that it is given to him.'

The elderly king nodded and took his leave. After paying his respects to the departing royal, an irritated Duryodhana ordered the footmen to lead the horses to the stables after placing the chariot inside with the other gifts. Then, with one longing backward glance, he strode towards the main palace. Yudhishthira would need to be informed of this lavish present.

The main palace of Indraprastha or the 'palace of illusion,' as people liked to call it, stood on a small hill at the centre of the sprawling royal compounds. It was higher and grander than any of the surrounding smaller palaces, covering almost three acres of red soil. Duryodhana walked on the stone-studded path leading to the front entrance, past lush, chirping gardens, rows of exotic trees he didn't recognise and flowing pools and streams of freshwater filled with swans and fragrant lotus flowers in myriad colours. In the distance sounded the melodic, almost tragic strains of a single veena, a string instrument, and flowers like queen of the night, lotus and marigolds amalgamated in the gardens, enveloping passers-by in their heady fragrance.

The front of the palace of illusions was towering, arching and undulating white stone, studded extravagantly with enormous murals of precious and semi-precious gems of every size and hue. Peacocks of turquoise and blue sapphire frolicked with deer of sandstone and tigers-eye. Ruby lotuses sat at the feet of marble maidens bedecked in real gold. Scenes of the hunt, prayer and festivity, scenes of gods and goddesses, resplendent courts, fierce battlefields and serene forests adorned the palace's imposing exterior. With each glance, it seemed a new detail would catch one's eye, be it a maiden with a pet mouse hidden in the folds of her lap or an archer in mid-battle shooting flowers instead of arrows. Such was the detail and intricacy of the palace that it was regarded, by all who laid eyes on it, as the largest work of art in the entire mortal world.

The entrance greeted Duryodhana icily, its grand, golden doors opening slowly, almost reluctantly, for him to pass through. Inside, Duryodhana encountered what never failed to strike him speechless. A crystal hall, with sinuous arches and beams that reflected, with their expertly crafted, glassy surfaces, the radiance of the outside sun. The hall and its visitor were bathed with brilliant, heatless light. Duryodhana looked around him. Intricate crystal lotuses grew in the floor, in the walls. Crystal clouds on the ceiling caught sunlight through small windows and shimmered like warm ice. He blinked and it seemed like the hall blinked back at him.

Much as Duryodhana's aesthetic senses were delighted by the crystal hall and its dancing daylight, a part of him couldn't help but feel chagrined at this display of wealth by his cousins. Yudhishthira and his brothers would do well to remember that Indraprastha, along with all its lands and subjects, was a gift to them by his father, Dhritarashtra, King of Hastinapur. To compete with the grandeur of Hastinapur was impolite, irreverent, even adharmic!

Duryodhana walked on, his mind conquered by familiar thoughts that had plagued him since he arrived at Indraprastha a week ago. Memories had torturously inundated his every waking moment; of him, his brothers and cousins when they were children, when they were teenagers training together under their guru, Dhronacharya. He replayed the day his father had bestowed a part of the kingdom to the five sons of his dead elder brother. An act Duryodhana had vehemently protested against. His father had consoled him, saying that the land his cousins had received was plagued by drought and barren as a hag.

Barren! Duryodhana now laughed humourlessly and shook his head. He had ridden to the fields outside Indraprastha last week to see for himself. They were flourishing! The palace servants had told him the farmers had methods of harvesting the scarce rainwater that fell to the ground. Witchcraft, his own servants had exclaimed with bright eyes and quivering lips. His manservant had even taken to marking his face with black *kohl* and burning incense with green chilli and lemons to ward off the evil eye.

Duryodhana strode towards the King's court, through breezy and lavishly styled ante-chambers filled with light. Servants, guards and courtiers bowed to him as he walked past them. His feet thumped loudly on the pearly white stone floor that was covered with inlaid murals of rubies, emeralds, crystals, turquoise and sapphire, reflecting much of the same gigantic artwork on the outer walls but with much more delicacy, detail and whimsy. The floor shone and shimmered unnaturally, almost as if there were a layer of water over it. Yet, it neither felt wet, nor slippery. He stepped over intricate designs made to look like carpets, depicting forest animals, birds and flowers, all in the most precious of gems.

As he walked, Duryodhana approached a large mural in one of the ante-chambers outside the women's quarters. It was a square design with a pond theme, depicting lotus flowers at the surface of clear water and fish and pond creatures in many colours underneath the surface. It shimmered and seemed to move just slightly under the bright reflection of sunlight. Duryodhana blinked. No wonder they called it the palace of illusions, he thought as he stepped over it.

An instant later, there was a great splash as his bulky frame tumbled face down in what was actually a pool of water. Duryodhana flailed in panic under the surface for a few seconds as he felt an airless clutch on his lungs. Then, his feet found the floor and he sheepishly emerged in the knee-deep pool, shaking his head wildly and sputtering.

A peal of laughter, high-pitched and spontaneous, rang in his drenched, horrified ears. He turned his head in its direction only to be confronted with Draupadi, Queen of Indraprastha, bent over and clutching her stomach as waves of laughter shook her body. She stood just outside the door to the royal women's wing and was oblivious to Duryodhana glaring at her with unconcealed fury. She saw only his person, dripping and frazzled like a wet cat, royal robes clinging to the folds of his oversized body and his crown floating a few feet away. Even his grand moustache drooped pathetically. The servants and handmaids, hovering around caught the infection of her laughter and suppressed giggles of delight by holding their hands over their quivering mouths. A few muffled coughs served to only infuriate Duryodhana further, as he felt the muscles in his throat start to twitch uncontrollably.

He clutched his robes and fished out his crown. His eyes never left Draupadi. Enraged though he was, he couldn't help but notice how her beauty had grown since he last saw her just after her marriage. No longer a maiden was she, but a woman, practised in all the arts and intricacies of women. Innocence was now a knowing eye, fear replaced by power.

Duryodhana felt a slight tug of attraction despite himself. He had tried to win Draupadi years ago at her *swayamvara*. His efforts had been in vain and his cousin Arjuna, Yudhishthira's younger brother, had been the one to succeed. Yet another victory for his cousins at his expense. He clenched his fists.

'Shrieking like a banshee suits you very little, Queen Draupadi,' said Duryodhana, his voice nasty.

'Soaking in that pool suits you even less, o' Prince Duryodhana,' Draupadi countered with delighted sarcasm. Her laughter renewed at her own witticism.

The spitfire. How he would like to be the master of her ... Duryodhana straightened his back and stepped out of the pool, trying to look as menacing as possible.

Draupadi's smile flickered for an instant but then her eyes lit up again. After all, how could she restrain herself when Duryodhana's clothes sloshed a trail of water behind him noisily as he approached. 'Do watch your step there, Prince Duryodhana. You may slip back in the pool again,' she laughed again as did the maids around her.

'Where I come from, not only is it unbecoming to laugh at a guest in one's home, it is considered indecent when a woman dares to laugh at a man. However, I suppose it must be quite usual in women with not one but five husbands. Excuse me o' Queen, for my ignorance in the habits of your ... kind,' said Duryodhana, his voice a hiss, mean and slick.

Draupadi stopped laughing. Duryodhana didn't know why, but it felt good to halt that carefree laughter. If it had belonged to him, perhaps he would have felt differently ... but no, it didn't belong to him. It belonged to his cousins.

Draupadi stood straight and said, in a haughty voice that had struck dumb many an insolent man in the past, 'It is because you are a guest in my home that I will tolerate what you have just dared to infer, o' Prince. Be mindful, however, that you are in the palace of one of the most powerful kings in the land.'

Duryodhana's voice came from behind clenched teeth, 'A king with a kingdom begotten by the charity of my father.'

Draupadi's eyes widened, 'Charity?' her voice was husky anger, 'You are in the mood to speak freely, o' prince, so I shall respond in kind. The only reason your father sits on the throne of Hastinapur is because of the charity of my husbands, who did not claim their rightful kingdom when their father, King Pandu died. Out of respect did they come here to Indraprastha, a barren land thrust upon them as poor compensation for their goodwill.'

She waved her hand around her, 'It took years of toil and hardship to build this city, to find ways to make the lands fertile and turn this bastard realm into a respectable kingdom. You and your father languished in the luxury of Hastinapur's palace for all of those years without so much as offering a helping hand. Only now, that Indraprastha is ripe with prosperity, do we enjoy the *pleasure* of your magnanimous company.'

Draupadi breathed heavily with agitation, 'It is because of my five husbands that you have a kingdom to inherit. You should thank them, o' Prince Duryodhana ...'

Duryodhana interrupted her, 'Thank them? Thank them for what, o' Queen? For an entire childhood of torment and humiliation? Should I thank Bhimsena, your precious husband, for beating me daily as we studied under the Guru Dronacharya? Should I thank Arjuna, your beloved husband, for shooting arrows at my feet as I danced to evade them? Or, perhaps I should thank the great and good Yudhishthira, your most senior husband, for never saying an unkind word to me while excusing his own brothers for their unkind words.'

Duryodhana spat bitterly on the ground, 'Year after year, I was told to be more like the heroic Pandava brothers. But no matter how hard I tried, I was always second best. I was even punished by the elders for complaining about their mistreatment of me. How could they be anything but the epitome of virtue? After all, they were the sons of the king, the heirs to the throse. And I, a mere cousin, destined to watch from the sidelines.'

He gathered his wet robes and leaned towards Draupadi one last time, 'So you will excuse me, o' Queen, if I don't feel sorry for their years of hardship in building this kingdom. You will excuse me if I didn't hand Hastinapur to your husbands on a platter for the taking.'

With that Duryodhana swung around and strode off towards the entrance, leaving Draupadi staring after him in bewilderment.

By the time he reached his apartments in one of the smaller palaces, Duryodhana was burning not only with rage but regret. He hadn't meant to say those things to Draupadi. He cursed his loose tongue as he slammed the giant door to his personal chamber. She would surely repeat his words to her husbands. The Pandavas would now know how he felt about them.

His manservant walked into the room and exclaimed in surprise. He hurried over to his master and began to strip him off the wet, offending robes. Duryodhana barely noticed. His thoughts had long abandoned his bodily discomforts and were now focusing on a more important matter at hand.

Duryodhana paced the floor as his manservant followed behind awkwardly, wiping his body with a dry cloth. He was sure the Pandavas would come after him now that the façade of cousinly love was cast aside. Questions raided his thoughts; would they try to influence his father against him with the help of the elders? Was his personal security at risk if he continued to stay here? And, the most crucial question of all; would they suspect that he was behind the attempts on their lives after their father had died?

Duryodhana felt a chill go down his spine as he recalled the events of that time many years ago. They had all just finished their education and returned to Hastinapur when the Pandavas lost their father, King Pandu, to a mysterious stroke in the forest. Young and inexperienced, they had allowed Dhritarashtra, their uncle, to take the throne after his elder brother's funeral.

It was then that Duryodhana, the new king's son, had made a vital ally. His maternal uncle, Shakuni, advised him to seize the opportunity fate had so kindly presented him by getting rid of the Pandavas once and for all. It would look like an accident, he said. Duryodhana would be crown prince, he said. Duryodhana would soon be king, he said. The words were like music to a young, previously ignored Duryodhana's ears. He could almost taste the power, feel the vast wealth of Hastinapur at his feet. He had agreed.

Shakuni's men had launched a series of murder attempts on the young Pandavas. Each time, it went horribly wrong. Their food was poisoned, only to be eaten by others. They were drugged and set in the river to drown, only to be rescued. Soon, they began to suspect that their lives were in danger. They staged their own death by setting their palace on fire one dark night and stealing away into the deep forest. Duryodhana's heart had leaped, albeit guiltily, when the burnt corpses of five men, planted by the Pandavas, had been removed from the charred remains the next morning. His day in the sun had finally arrived. But that day had been short-lived. A few years later, the Pandavas had emerged from nowhere, grown men. They had spent their years in hiding well, wandering disguised as priests from kingdom to kingdom, learning about politics, warfare and life. Most crucially, they had developed alliances with powerful kings. Draupadi had been by their side, a wife shared by all five of them.

Duryodhana recalled the shock of seeing the Pandavas after years of thinking them dead. They had changed since he had known them. Gone were the teasing bullies, the spoiled heirs. Gone were the light-hearted laughs and superior eyes. Hard men and skilled warriors, they eyed him with suspicion and were polite to a fault. Politer still were they to Dhritarashtra, from whom they demanded their share of the kingdom....

A loud rattle outside the chamber brought Duryodhana's thoughts back to the present. His manservant quickly brushed off the last crease on the fresh robes he had wrapped around his master and opened the large chamber door. On the other side was Shakuni, banging the golden tip of his elaborately carved, wooden cane against the marble floor. An ugly, tired looking man was Duryodhana's maternal uncle, sallow skinned, thin and craggy with his sparse, greying hair and bent spine. As he walked into the room, Duryodhana got a whiff of his scent, stale smoke and pungent incense oil combined with sweat that was always in attendance no matter how cool the weather. It was not a scent Duryodhana held in regard, but time had made it familiar.

Shakuni's eyes scanned Duryodhana from head to toe. They were the only part of him that was energetic and bright even as Duryodhana found their piercing stare a little disconcerting.

'I heard there was an accident in the palace,' said Shakuni as he motioned for Duryodhana's manservant to leave and sat down with difficulty on a divan.

Duryodhana sat opposite him on a large stool and said with studied nonchalance, 'I fell into a pool of water.'

Shakuni nodded, mirroring the false casualness of Duryodhana's stance. 'You are not hurt I see. That is fortunate,' he said.

Duryodhana rubbed his temples as he felt a muscle begin to twitch near his left eye, 'Yes.' He contemplated the floor.

Shakuni moved his head as if to look around the room but his gaze never left his nephew. After a moment, he said in a soft voice, 'The queen Draupadi was present, I am told.'

The twitch worsened. Duryodhana said irritably, 'Yes, she was. It happened outside the women's quarters.' He looked up at his uncle, 'What of it?'

Shakuni shrugged his shoulders, shook his head with a look of complete innocence and said, 'Nothing at all, my child. I am merely glad to see that my beloved nephew is unhurt and well.' He started to stand up, 'I just came to put my mind at ease. Now, I will be on my way,' he struggled determinedly to alight from the divan.

Duryodhana quickly stood and motioned for his uncle to remain seated. He had not meant to be curt. He sat next to Shakuni on the divan and, after a few moments, said with a bent head, 'I said some things to her.'

Shakuni's small smile was unseen by his nephew. He asked with concern in his voice, 'To whom?'

'To Draupadi.' Duryodhana looked up with worry in his eyes, 'I told her about ... about how the Pandavas had treated me and ... that they got their kingdom because of my father's charity.'

Shakuni looked at Duryodhana with silent reproach.
Duryodhana erupted.

'She laughed at me! She dared ... to mock me!' He stood up
and started to pace the room, 'That indecent woman, husbanded
by five men. She is no more than a ... a prostitute! For such
an adharmic woman to insult me was unbearable, Uncle.'

Shakuni nodded and said, 'Yes. It must have been disagreeable
to hear mocking words from the mouth of one so fallen in
morality. Still, we must be careful not to offend the Pandavas.
They have powerful allies.'

Duryodhana looked at the elaborate ceiling in exasperation,
'But of course! Who can forget that now that the Rajasuya
sacrifice has been conducted. *Emperor*, he calls himself now. Of
all of them, I thought Yudhishthira might have been blessed
with the least immodest attributes. I was wrong, obviously. Did
you see how he invited Krishna, King of the Vaishnavas, to
sit next to him throughout the week's proceedings? His own
brothers were not accorded that privilege. It is to be expected
that all the other kings would follow Krishna in allying with
them now. Krishna is the most powerful of them all. At least, he
has the humility not to declare himself emperor!' His forehead
ticked furiously as he turned to Shakuni.

'They are clever, these Pandavas,' said Shakuni, 'They have
cultivated their relationship with Krishna very carefully over the
years. They know his support will guarantee them a powerful
kingdom.'

'And riches,' Duryodhana waved his hand towards the
window, 'Ever since I have arrived here, I have been inundated
with the most glorious wealth of every kind. Their coffers
are bursting with gold and precious stones, their stables with
horses and elephant yards with the most magnificent of beasts.
Their fields are ripe with sweet fruit and grain and the people

dressed in fine cloth. The palaces . . .,' he pointed at the carved, inlaid ceiling with tears stabbing at his eyes, 'are . . . there are no words to describe them.'

Duryodhana sat down again, despondent, 'Even the gifts I have received on their behalf during the Rajasuya have been magnificent. The finest of cloth, the rarest of stones. Exotic breeds of beasts have been added to their collection and chariots . . . chariots of gold!' He rubbed his ticking forehead, 'I have never even dreamt of such riches. Hastinapur pales in comparison.'

He was silent for a moment. Then he said, in a weak voice, 'It is unfair, o' Uncle. No matter how hard I try, they always best me.'

Shakuni was deep in thought. His thin frame seemed listless but his fingers furiously rubbed the smooth handle of his cane. Then, they stopped. Shakuni, looking very pleased, leaned over and patted Duryodhana on his shoulder, 'You are despondent for no reason, my child. This could all be yours, if you wanted it so.'

Duryodhana looked up at his uncle quickly, his expression a mix of confusion and anticipation.

Shakuni smiled a smile of self-satisfaction, 'How would you like to be the lord of both Hastinapur and Indraprastha?'

Duryodhana waved his hand and turned away dismissively, 'That is impossible! You dream fruitlessly, o' Uncle. Indraprastha is inconquerable, especially after this Rajasuya. Yudhishthira is too powerful. Krishna will be . . .'

Shakuni interrupted softly, 'I wasn't about to suggest we try and conquer Indraprastha, my child. That would be extremely foolhardy.'

Duryodhana turned back, his interest piqued, 'Then how . . . ?'

Shakuni leaned back on the divan. He fingered his cane coyly, 'Your old uncle has a few tricks of his own.'

Duryodhana shrugged in irritation, 'Your attempts to help me with your 'tricks' in the past were not only unsuccessful, but almost led to my downfall. If I had been discovered as the source of those assassination attempts, the Pandavas would not have spared my life,' He got up and began to pace slowly, 'It is better that I live with my thoughts, rather than tempt death.'

Shakuni said softly, 'If you are afraid of the Pandavas, then I understand ...'

Duryodhana swung around, eyes wide, his bulky frame heaving, his hairs on end like a wild hound. His voice was loud, confrontational, 'Afraid? I am a warrior, afraid of no one! What is it you suggest? Tell me now!' He put his fists on hips and stood, legs apart, facing his uncle. It was a dramatic stance, designed to intimidate.

Shakuni almost smiled again, but composed his face too quickly for Duryodhana to notice. His response was meek, placating, 'Patience, my child. My plan is foolproof. Your life will be in no danger. In fact, Yudhishthira will hand over Indraprastha and all its riches to you himself.'

Duryodhana's stance relaxed as a surge of possibility filled him. He could feel the riches, the power. He inched closer involuntarily, 'How can you arrange that?'

Shakuni held up his bony, wrinkled hands, 'With these two hands,' he looked at the appendages now with a contemplative expression and said, almost to himself, 'Hands that were deemed unfit in combat, ugly in matrimony, inept in artistry.' Shakuni's eyes were still as he murmured softly, 'Dark hands ...'

Duryodhana sighed dramatically in exasperation, 'Uncle, you tease me. Tell me of your plan.'

Shakuni looked back at his nephew in obvious enjoyment of the suspense he had created, 'I will. But first, tell me, my beloved nephew, how would you thank your old uncle if he placed Indraprastha at your feet?'

So there it was. The inevitable condition. Duryodhana's mouth hardened, 'What is it you wish as payment?'

Shakuni ignored Duryodhana's expression. His eyes were alight with excitement, 'An army. The biggest, most powerful army in the known world. At my command.' He looked at his nephew, 'You will have the power, as king of Hastinapur and Indraprastha, to demand allegiance from kings. You can amass an army of legendary proportions.'

Duryodhana frowned in curiosity, 'You want an army? To march against whom?'

Shakuni became a little guarded, 'That, you will find out in time, my beloved nephew. Do I have your word?'

Duryodhana's curiosity was fired further, 'Tell me against whom, o' Uncle and I shall give you my word.'

Shakuni frowned. He disliked bargaining but he was so close . . . he relented, 'Against Gandhahar.'

Duryodhana was taken aback. Gandhahar was Shakuni's native home. It was where he grew up along with Duryodhana's mother, Gandhari. It was where his elder brother now ruled as king. From what Duryodhana knew, the relations between Shakuni and his brother had always been cordial despite the fact that Shakuni had moved to Hastinapur with his sister when she married Dhritarashtra many decades ago.

As a child, Duryodhana had often asked his uncle why he chose to live in his brother-in-law's kingdom and not his native Gandhahar, a faraway land in the north-west mountains. It was the weather in Hastinapur, Shakuni replied, sometimes, humid and pleasant compared to the rugged, chilly drought of

Gandhahar. It was affection for his sister Gandhari, was the reply other times, even though Duryodhana knew that they barely spoke. Shakuni always provided an appropriate answer. Whether there was more to his uncle's decision, Duryodhana never knew, but he did know that Shakuni was unlike every other person he had ever met from Gandhahar. Its people were tall, fair-complexioned and well-built, skilled in warfare, music and producing crop from their harsh, mountainous lands. Fearless, proud in stature and loud in voice were Gandhahari people, their honest laughter as quick as their violent temper. His uncle Shakuni was nothing like them.

Duryodhana said, with little tact, 'Why?'

Shakuni's eyes flashed anger even as his body remained limp, 'It is not for you to ask why, nephew. Do I have your word?' His voice then softened, 'If I make you the richest, most powerful king in the land ...'

Duryodhana took a deep breath. He saw the wealth and felt the power once again. They felt so close he could almost touch them.

Duryodhana looked around him at the ornate chamber. He immediately dismissed any thought about the morality of Shakuni's plan to gain Indraprastha or the welfare of the Pandavas. Had they treated him with a little concern to begin with, his wrath needn't have fallen upon them.

He thought about his father, who would surely object to his son invading Gandhahar, one of their strongest allies. Duryodhana shrugged the thought away. He would persuade his father when the time came.

His only concern was his mother and how she would feel, her childhood home invaded, her family imprisoned, maybe even murdered. He looked at his uncle, unable to admit to the weakness of considering a woman's emotions, even if she was his mother. His will battled his weakness.

Shakuni read Duryodhana's conflict instantly. He continued softly, 'If I make you the master of not only all the residents of Indraprastha, but also of its queen ...'

Every inch of Duryodhana's body tensed. He heard Draupadi's laughter, her demeaning words. He saw her haughty face, her flashing eyes and proud chin. His fury returned. She should have known better than to cross him. He would be the master of her. He would make her pay ten-fold for today's humiliation. He would show the world that she was nothing more than a common whore.

He looked at Shakuni, 'I give you my word.'

DRAUPADI'S SUBMISSION

'*No!*' she screamed, as her lungs constricted and her heart galloped. She felt a sharp ringing in her ears and then, nothing, as she succumbed gratefully to the blackness.

When she awoke, Princess Draupadi was on her maiden bed in her chambers, droplets of rosewater trickling down from a drenched cloth on her forehead onto the silken pillow. Above her, hovered Neela, her chief handmaiden and the palace women with worried expressions on their faces. For a moment, she wondered what all the fuss was about. Then, she remembered.

Draupadi moaned like an animal in pain and broke down, tears bursting forth as violent sobs racked her small body. She curled like a foetus on the bed, her drenched eyes against her knees. A few of the distraught handmaidens sobbed along in sympathy. Others petted and stroked Draupadi's hair and heaving shoulders. Neela stood silently, looking at the princess as one would, towards a dying child. It was so unfair, she thought.

Outside, drums rolled and conches called out relentlessly, belting out sounds that lifted the hearts of the kingdom's subjects. Weeks of excited anticipation had passed and the time for unbridled celebration had finally arrived. The people of Panchala geared themselves for feasting and festivity. Excited yelps were heard on the streets as courtiers distributed new clothing and sweetmeats to the poor, hawkers roamed the lanes selling oil lamps and incense with knowing grins and extra-loud voices, and giggling girls crowded in street corners only to be shooed back to their housework by vigilant hags. The air in the marketplace was pure energy, infused with the scents of fresh cardamom, clarified butter and caramelised jaggery. The kingdom was ripe with excitement, with activity.

The royal women's wing of the palace had been much like that yesterday. Yesterday, the women had laughed with abandon. They had filled copper pots and plates with red ochre and flowers, hung fresh strings of mango leaves over doorways, wrapped hundreds of presents in silk and gold cloth and bought trinkets by the dozens from eunuch vendors. They had sung songs and clapped in unison as the eunuchs broke into spontaneous dancing. In the evening, they had bathed the hallways, courtyards and windows in the shimmering light of hundreds of oil lamps and huddled in groups, whispering and giggling excitedly as they nudged each other with knowing looks.

Today, however, it was as though a death were being mourned. The courtyards, peppered with spent oil lamps, wilting flowers and a few despondent mango leaves, were abandoned. No song or laugh was to be heard. Even the usually happy clink of jewelry and swish of sarees as the women moved around seemed to resonate dully today. Eyes darted surreptitiously toward Princess Draupadi's chambers and the hiss of muted whispers echoed in the hallways as the wind carried it from far corners.

Hours earlier, the doors to Draupadi's chambers had been banged shut in haste so none outside could attend to the raw sound of her weeping. Now, the doors opened once again and Princess Draupadi ran out, her saree askew, her hair wild and loose, her eyes swollen and red, with streams of black kohl running down her cheeks. She looked anxious and upset, yet purposeful. Ignoring the stares of the women around, she raced pagan-like towards the guest chambers of the royal ladies. Neela and the other handmaidens appeared next, running out in utter confusion. She called out to Draupadi and followed suit but they were too far behind. The princess, swifter and more agile than most of her servants, had reached the entrance to the guest chambers, slammed the doors shut and locked them from within.

Once inside, Draupadi clutched the wall and took a deep breath as she gasped, waves of dizziness washing over her. She had to stay on her feet, she had to act quickly. This was her last . . . no, her only resort. She walked hurriedly towards the bedchamber, her heart racing. The distinct odour of betel nut, strong and acrid, hung in the air. It grew stronger as she approached the bedchamber. Draupadi looked inside and saw the silhouette of a middle-aged woman lounging on a divan next to a window chewing betel leaves. This woman, dressed in the simple white saree of a widow, looked pensively at the garden outside while she removed the leaves, one by one, from a gilded box and placed them into deep orange stained lips that had begun to wrinkle with age.

The woman turned towards Draupadi as she entered the bedchamber. Her unadorned face, plump and of plain complexion, gave neither confirmation nor contradiction of former beauty. Her features could best be described as neat, giving no offense or inspiration. Her frame was portly, yet she held herself with dignity, her air one of deliberation, restraint and the latent authority of the elderly.

She smiled slightly but no compassion reached her eyes as she beheld the distraught Draupadi, who stood near the door. She put down the box, patted the divan and said in a high-pitched, soft voice, 'Come and sit, Princess.'

Draupadi looked upon her impassive face, colourless apart from the slash of orange, and felt utterly desperate. Her face contorted with fresh tears as she ran and quickly sunk to the floor next to the divan, burying her face and hands in the woman's feet. Her voice was a mere squeak, 'O queen, I come to you not as a princess but as a beggar.'

Kunti, former queen of Hastinapur looked at the top of Draupadi's unadorned head, the thick strands of her long hair sweeping the stone floor and her violently heaving shoulders with mild irritation. She patted her head with an awkward hand, an act that seemed only to fuel Draupadi's weeping. Kunti then looked around, as if to search in vain for someone to take over, before muttering, 'Stop crying and sit up, please.'

Draupadi looked up at Kunti, whose gaze fell upon her own feet, now wet and stained with oily, smudged kohl from Draupadi's eyes. She stiffened. Draupadi, noticing Kunti's distaste, frantically reached for her saree to wipe the stains but instead, knocked the betel leaf box with her hand and sent it crashing to the floor. Kunti watched its contents tumble out and land solemnly on the stone. Her voice had distaste in it when she spoke, 'Come now, princess. Do away with this ... this state of yours and speak in a manner befitting your station.'

Draupadi reeled in surprise from the sharp words but a part of her realised that she would not be heard unless she composed herself. So, forcing her tears back she resolutely wiped her face with her saree and stopped sniffing but continued to sit on the floor, looking up at Kunti with large eyes. She didn't know this woman well, but felt sure she would help if she could only be made to understand....Her voice was husky, cracked from hours of crying, 'O queen, I have always been a motherless child. When I met you yesterday and saw the infinite love you have for your five sons, I felt I too could have a mother at last.' She paused, 'May I call myself your daughter?'

Kunti's reply was trite, 'Yes. A daughter-in-law is always considered the equal of a daughter.' She leaned back a little, her eyes straying from Draupadi's, her palms crossing over her knees. She looked mildly annoyed, as if she was being compelled to attend to this needless conversation.

Draupadi could sense Kunti's withdrawal but she felt fuelled, by desperation, to continue, 'O queen . . . o' mother. Is it not the duty of a mother to protect her daughter's honour?'

Kunti was silent for a few moments. Then, she said in a measured tone, 'It is the mother's duty to do what is best for her children.'

There was a gentle knock on the doors of the outside chamber. Draupadi started. Time was running out.

Outside the guest chambers, Neela stood within a chaotic group of royal women. Each had something to say about the situation. It was lamented by some that Draupadi must be possessed by a demon while others argued that she had, in her hysteria, completely lost all sense of conduct by locking herself into her future mother-in-law's chambers. They deliberated over the reaction of her father, King Drupada, when he found out that Draupadi was trying to talk to Queen Kunti about the situation. He would be livid, most of them agreed.

Amidst the commotion, Neela knocked softly on the door, with a feeble hope that Draupadi might open the door. When expected silence answered back, she stood quietly, trying to force her mind to think about the best course of action.

Suddenly, a hush fell over the group. Coming towards them was a petite, fair-complexioned, young woman dressed extravagantly in the finest of royal regalia. Her saree was one of saffron-coloured silk embroidered with gold leaves and the jewelry she wore, right from her elaborate gold belt with dozens of tinkling rubies that fell upon her thin hips to her oversized golden nose ring with a dazzling ruby at its base, was almost blinding in its excessiveness. Her doll-like, girlish face, artfully aided by copious amounts of kohl, ochres and oils, had sharp cheekbones, thin lips and an aristocratic nose. Her light brown eyes were alight with enjoyment as she walked towards the group.

She waved a fair, lazy hand at Neela, who stiffened but reluctantly stepped forward, hands folded in supplication. 'So, your mistress is to be married at last. And, what a marriage it is to be,' she said with high-pitched, contemptuous pleasure, 'Tell me, where is that feisty sister-in-law of mine? I must congratulate her. It is not every day that a princess can call herself the promised wife of one Kuru king, let alone five!' she giggled breathlessly in over-excitement.

Neela gritted her teeth as she looked upon the floor. The woman stopped giggling and said in her high-pitched, haughty voice, 'Speak handmaiden. Answer my question or I shall have you whipped.'

Neela's answer was forced, 'She is in the guest chambers, o' Princess.'

Princess Chaya started abruptly. She frowned, 'Why?'

Neela knew not what to say but instinctively thought to protect Draupadi as best as she could. So she lied, 'She was summoned by our guest.'

Chaya looked at Neela with suspicion. 'It is not the norm for girls to have private conference with their mothers-in-law before the marriage ceremony. Does my husband, Prince Dhrishtadyumna, know about this?' she said, almost to herself.

All the women hung their heads in silence.

Chaya walked up to the door of Queen Kunti's chambers and was about to knock on the door when Neela interrupted, 'Our guest may not like to be disturbed.'

Princess Chaya stopped with her fist in mid-air and stepped back in indecision. It would be inappropriate for her, a young princess, to interrupt a queen's conference. On the other hand, what was Draupadi doing in there? Something was distinctly suspicious. She concentrated upon the expressions of the women around her, frowning her suspicions, looking for dishonesty, for a sign that her timely intervention would, in fact, be welcomed and not undesirable. She found no such comfort. Each face was suddenly set in bland stone, staring back at her unblinkingly.

'Fruitless will this misplaced loyalty to that wild girl be. You shall see!' She said as she turned and hurried away.

Neela watched Chaya striding towards the main wing of the palace with dread in her heart.

The floor was cold under her thin saree and a prickling sensation had begun to creep up Draupadi's legs. They would be numb soon, but she didn't think of moving them. Her mind was racing. She had tried appealing to Kunti for help without any success. Perhaps if she tried reasoning with her, the widow queen might be more forthcoming.

'Mother Kunti . . . ,' Draupadi leaned forward, 'It is men who rule our society and preside over its scriptures. A man may do as he pleases as long as he is able to justify it as a dharmic action. A woman must live by the dharma prescribed to her by men. And, dharma is unforgiving of women. Any . . . unusual act by a woman can be misunderstood by men ... it can even be called adharmic by the judgemental,' she paused, hopefully.

Kunti's face gave no indication of having understood her meaning.

Draupadi felt frustrated. This impassive woman who sat before her, who pretended not to understand her, was the reason she was in this situation at all. Had it not been for her words ... her fateful words.

Draupadi remembered the moment they had been uttered. She had stood at the door of a priest's hut, on the outskirts of Panchala, with the man who had won her hand in marriage at her *Swayamwara*. She had known not his name or anything about him at that time but had thought him a suspiciously warrior-like travelling priest, with his shaved head and white tunic. Her suspicions were soon proved accurate. Now, she knew that it had been Prince Arjuna of Hastinapur, in disguise, who had won her hand, a prince widely thought to have perished with his brothers and mother in a palace fire in Hastinapur. Behind her in the hut had stood his elder brother, who must have been Prince Bhimsena, a very tall, muscular man with the large, protruding stomach common to men who enjoy their sweetmeats. Inside the door had been the eldest brother, whom she knew now was Prince Yudhishthira, a thin man of medium complexion and weak chin. Outside the hut and deep in conversation were the youngest brothers, who were surely Prince Nakula and Prince Sahadeva, identical twins with fair, boyish features and a good deal of mischief in their eyes.

Draupadi, who had no clue about their disguise at that time, had stood at the hut door shivering with exhaustion in her royal regalia, crown atop her head. None of the brothers had spoken to her during the two-hour walk from the palace but Bhimsena had kept glancing awkwardly in her direction, as if she were a bizarre animal he knew not how to conduct. The twins had walked at some distance behind them, gossiping and laughing as they replayed the events at the *swayamwara*. Yudhishthira had walked slightly ahead, his eyes stoically fixed on the path, ignoring her presence, his lips pursed together righteously. Only Arjuna had met her eyes with his own as they had walked side-by-side, her head held high despite the scorching pain in her naked feet as they touched the hot earth. Her brow had dripped with sweat for the first time as she trudged in her unwieldy finery under a sun that struggled to overpower even as twilight forced it to retreat. Arjuna's eyes had been amused yet approving of her spirit. They had also been aroused, a fact she had impossibly tried to ignore.

One of the brothers, she couldn't recall which one, had laughingly called out upon approaching the dwelling, 'Mother! Look what alms we have collected for you today.'

From behind the hut, where a wooden stove spat loud sparks as a stick wrestled inside it, had come Kunti's impatient voice, 'Well, let it be divided among the five of you equally.'

Draupadi remembered how the brothers had frozen, unsure of what to do next. She remembered glancing into each of their faces. The twins watched their elder brothers, a laugh ready to erupt from their twitching mouths. Arjuna had looked shocked and worried. Bhimsena had looked scared, almost like a naughty child caught in the act of stealing. Yudhishthira was the only one who had been nonplussed. He had looked straight at her, his face unreadable. Draupadi had the impression that his mind raced with thought even as his expression was studiously impassive.

Of all the brothers, Draupadi now thought fleetingly, Kunti's expressions most resembled those of her eldest son.

She tried again, imploring Kunti with her eyes as she spoke, 'Mother, would you want your daughter to be called adharmic? Would you want your son to be married to a woman who is labelled immoral?' Tears stung her eyes but she held them back, 'For they would surely . . .'

Kunti interrupted firmly, 'Princess, it is not my wish to see you or any other woman labelled as adharmic. However, destiny is the wish of the gods. We are powerless to influence that which is pre-ordained.'

Draupadi felt her ready temper bubble up inside her and took a deep breath to quell it. She was getting desperate now and harsh words would not help her cause. She whispered, 'Mother, destiny can be changed. It would take just one word from you . . .'

Kunti's eyes flashed. She said coldly, 'My words have already been spoken.'

Neela watched with horror as Princess Chaya walked quickly back towards them with Queen Soudamini in tow. Queen Soudamini, a kindly, if slightly eccentric, middle-aged woman struggled to keep up with her step-daughter-in-law's hurried strides. Soudamini's health was poor and she spent most of her time in prayer and meditation, far removed from the goings-on in the women's wing. Her hair, now almost completely grey, fell upon her back in a frizzy downpour and the kohl that lined her eyes was so deeply embedded in every wrinkle, it gave her an almost owlish look. She looked harassed, as if unwilling but compelled to do an undesirable task assigned to her.

Chaya was talking to her husband's stepmother in a loud, quick voice, 'My husband had no idea about this . . . this conference. He and King Drupada think it is highly inappropriate, especially since everything has already been decided and preparations for the marriage ceremony have started. The princess might say something to offend our guest and where would that leave us? That is why they have asked you to intervene.'

Soudamini was out of breath as she replied, 'Don't you think we may be overreacting? The queen Kunti may have summoned the princess to explain the situation. I don't see why I have to....'

'But you must!' Chaya interrupted, with some violence in her tone, 'It is a question of the princess's reputation. Of the kingdom's reputation! My husband says that queen Kunti was most happy with the arrangement. He says that she was the one who insisted on it even when the others were in doubt. She is very particular about dharma and would not allow her words, uttered albeit in haste when her sons brought Draupadi to their hut yesterday, to be in vain. She has no reason to summon the princess, my husband says. She would not do anything that is against the prescribed norm. My husband says...'

Soudamini let out an exasperated sigh, 'Alright, alright,' she rubbed her temples as she halted outside the chamber doors.

She looked upon Neela and smiled slightly, 'Handmaiden, you are princess Draupadi's companion. What is your name?'

Neela smiled back. She had known Draupadi's step-mother since she was a child but the absent-minded queen never remembered her name. In fact, she sometimes had trouble remembering the names of her own children. She bowed, hands folded, 'Neela is my name, o' queen.'

'Neela,' Soudamini said kindly, 'Do you know why your mistress is visiting our guest? Was she summoned or did she seek conference with queen Kunti of her own volition?'

Princess Chaya interrupted quickly, glaring at Neela, 'Do not waste time on these handmaidens, o' queen-mother. They know not what is proper and decent for those of us who are royalty.'

Neela avoided Chaya's gaze for fear that her dislike of the young princess may be evident. She looked instead at queen Soudamini, pleading silently with her eyes, willing the old queen to protect her stepdaughter. Soudamini had never been a very involved parent, leaving the care of her children and stepchildren to the women of the palace. She and Draupadi shared an affectionate relationship but as Draupadi grew into a woman and her independent and assertive personality began to reveal itself, Soudamini had stayed out of her way. She was never the one to confront or create conflict.

Now, as Soudamini looked at Neela, she saw in the handmaiden's eyes a veiled message and a cry for help. Draupadi had obviously not been summoned at all. She had, like she always did, taken matters into her own hands without thought for the consequences. Intervening now would ensure that Draupadi would be put in her place and the marriage would take place as planned. Letting Draupadi stay in the guest chambers any longer may lead to a misunderstanding between the two kingdoms and perhaps even war, should the fiery princess insult the queen Kunti. On the other hand, Draupadi, if given more time, may be able to miraculously convince Kunti to change her mind about the marriage. Soudamini's thoughts overwhelmed her. And yet, she had to do something.

Kunti's expression bordered on disgust. She stood and walked towards the window, turning her back on Draupadi. She spoke as if to a servant girl, who knew neither the rules of social conduct nor understood the importance of the scriptures, 'A mother's word is sacred to her children. They must carry out her bidding without question or their practice of dharma is invalid. Should my words not be made true by my sons, it would destroy not only my dharma, by making me a liar, but also that of my sons.'

Draupadi had had enough. She had pleaded, reasoned and even tried to appeal to this woman's obviously absent sense of womanly compassion. Never in her life had she encountered a person who seemed more like a stone wall than a living being. She could not hold back any longer as she felt the crash of rage break her already flimsy dam of self-control, 'What about my dharma?' she shouted as she staggered to her feet, 'Did no one care at all about what would be said of me if I were to marry all your sons? How is that even possible? Do you ask that my body, worshipped by my father's subjects, pampered since birth by my handmaidens and untouched by any man, now succumb to five men?' she waved her hands wildly as she inched closer to Kunti, her shrill voice resounding off the walls, 'I would rather jump into the holy river and drown myself for even that would be a better destiny than this. At least, I would die a princess, not a prostitute,' her tirade ended in a high-pitched shriek.

Kunti had, at first, looked surprised at this unexpected outburst by her future daughter-in-law. Now, as Draupadi finished her diatribe, she saw Kunti with an expression she had never before seen. There was no mask of impassivity, no awkwardness with impropriety. Her eyes were hard as stone and her lips pressed so tight they could cut like a sword. She grabbed Draupadi by her arms and shook her before saying, through her teeth, in a harsh voice, 'There is very little difference between the two, Princess Draupadi. If you had a mother she would have taught you that. Since you don't and I have been put in the unfortunate position of being a mother to you, here is my first lesson. Princesses are good for two things; to give birth to future kings and to be political pawns. The sooner you accept this, the happier you will be,' Kunti's eyes blazed with anger as she spoke, 'My father married me to a sickly, impotent man who loved another and made me act outside our marriage to give birth to each of my sons. It wasn't exactly what I wanted either, but I did it, not only for the sake of lineage but so that I would not be a virgin widow, discarded after his almost certain death.' She paused, her chest heaving, her gaze breaking away. She let go of Draupadi and took a deep breath, turning her back upon the princess. Then, she said, in a raw voice, 'So, heed my words, princess. As long as you marry according to your father's wishes, you will be useful. Otherwise, you're just another woman, a burden upon men and utterly disposable.'

Draupadi barely registered the banging of the chamber doors. She was too deeply focused on Kunti's words to pay attention. 'Does my father indeed wish this upon me?' she whispered.

Kunti let out a bitter laugh, 'He wishes to be allied with the Pandavas. As long as the priests sanction this union, his reputation is safe. Your feelings upon the matter are the merest consideration.' She looked with hard pity at Draupadi.

Draupadi felt shattered. No woman had ever before spoken to her like that, spelled out so certainly what she had but vaguely perceived till now. She had spent a lifetime trying to prove herself as worthy as her brother Dhrishtadyumna of her father's affection. While Dhrishtadyumna had indulged in mindless excesses, Draupadi had mastered the scriptures, astronomy and the arts, trained in warfare and learnt diligently the craft of governance and administration. She had even studied curative treatments for human ailments, an exact science practised by a handful of men in the kingdom. Yet, she had spent year after year tucked away in the women's wing while Dhrishtadyumna presided over the kingdom with her father in court. In the end, she now thought bitterly, she was nothing more than the mares in her father's stables, worth only as much as her womb and the bloodline it could continue.

Draupadi looked at the hardened, bitter woman in front of her. She felt no anger towards Kunti anymore. There was just one question left in her mind, 'And you? Why do you want this, o' queen?'

The door of the chamber rattled again. Draupadi heard her stepmother's voice outside shout, 'Queen Kunti. May I enter?'

Kunti took one last look at Draupadi and sighed. Her voice was milder, even slightly apologetic, 'If only Arjuna desired you, there would be no need for this. But, you are very beautiful, Princess Draupadi, and it is important for me to keep my sons together. If divided, they would fall easily into the hands of their enemies.'

Kunti turned, walked outside to the chamber doors and opened them to let a flustered Soudamini and an eager Chaya inside. She smiled as if nothing were amiss and politely asked them to be seated.

Draupadi stood alone in the middle of the bedchamber. She remembered Yudhishthira's expression when his mother's words were uttered. Had there been desire in those eyes as they had stared at her? Had Kunti seen something in her sons' expressions when she had walked into the hut and realised her mistake? Confused, apologetic exclamations had soon turned into thoughtful silence before she welcomed Draupadi and continued the day's work as if nothing extraordinary had occurred.

It didn't matter now, Draupadi thought. Kunti had made it clear she would not intervene to stop the marriage. Her choices were clear now. She could either accept her fate or drown herself in the holy Ganga river. Were she to run away, her father would surely have her brought back, maybe, even killed for dishonouring him. Draupadi's eyes stung as she thought about her father. What would he think if she were to kill herself? Would he be sorry for his selfishness, regret his decision or wish that he had done things differently? Probably not. If anything he would think she was a coward, unworthy of warrior lineage, and disown her.

The thought of instigating her own death was distasteful. Warriors were taught that death without honour was the worst possible thing and would guarantee an eternity spent in the realm of demons.

Draupadi was not afraid of demons. But, above all things, she was not a coward. Given the choice between being called a prostitute and a coward, she would rather face the former. A prostitute at least had honour.

She heard Kunti's soft voice exchanging pleasantries with Soudamini in the other chamber. She could also hear Princess Chaya clearing her throat loudly. Draupadi's hands went to her face and began to wipe away the tracks of kohl on her cheeks. She would not give Chaya the satisfaction of seeing her bowed in humiliation. She would not give anyone that satisfaction. If to run away or drown herself was to be weak, then she would stay. Let the world rail at her, she would stare them down. No one would ever dare to call Draupadi weak. If this be her destiny, then so be it.

Draupadi wiped her eyes with her saree and tied her unkempt hair into a firm knot. Then, shoulders pulled back, she strode into the outside chamber.

Soudamini saw Draupadi emerge from the bedchamber. Although her eyes were swollen red and her saree stained with kohl, she showed no outward signs of emotion as she quietly walked towards them. On seeing her, Kunti smiled and said, 'Come and be seated with us, princess. I was just telling Queen Soudamini how much I have enjoyed your company.'

Soudamini held her breath as her stepdaughter gazed into Kunti's eyes for one long moment before she folded her hands, bowed and sat demurely at her future mother-in-law's feet. Her eyes blank, she stared ahead into the distance. Soudamini blinked back her tears and swallowed the lump rising in her throat and politely addressed Kunti, 'You must try our cardamom sweetmeats after the ceremony tomorrow, Queen Kunti. The kingdom of Panchala is famous for them.'

KUNTI'S SUBMERSION

She afternoon sun blazed his disapproval upon her. Amidst harsh gasps Princess Kunti glared right back at him. Defiant eyes belied the trained face. She didn't allow herself the indulgence of loud wrath. That was for the peasants, her old tutor had said when she was a young girl. The women of the zenana, royal women, never revealed themselves in so vulgar a manner. They were expected to behave with dignity, with grace. With silence.

And, Princess Kunti was the very embodiment of a royal woman. Dignified and graceful. Silent.

Frail and of unexceptional complexion, her plain face was defined by that look of helplessness, of dependency, that fired the protective hearts and tyrannical wills of men. It was her only claim to womanly beauty and she had cultivated it well.

Her adoptive father, King Kuntibhoja, had in fact, once likened her to the very river water that was lapping insistently on her ankle at this very moment. The river water, he said, flowed easily along its prescribed route, never questioning direction or destination, obedient to the unyielding riverbed and forceful currents. It was a correct, if incomplete, observation. Kunti had indeed always flowed easily for she knew it pleased the man she called Father. And, as long as he was pleased, she was his beloved daughter. As long as he was pleased, she was a princess. Yes, Kunti had always flowed easily, obediently. Until now.

Her knees almost gave way as she sank upon a slippery rock on the shallow bank. Its bright green mould, kept wet and loose by the constant ebb and flow of the river, stained her white saree, mixing and melting with the red of her blood until dirty mustard blotches emerged from their consummation. A sharp, female pain forced her to kneel on the riverbed instead. She ignored the tiny needle-like pebbles digging into her kneecaps as the agony of more bloody afterbirth, surging from between her legs, punished her exhausted body once more.

But the pain of guilt was far worse than its physical cousin. It flooded parts of her body beyond her reach or comprehension. She refused to buckle against its vicious tide, her will pushing her weak body to grasp the precious air. She needed precious air to keep moving. To do what she must to stay alive. To keep her son alive.

It had been the Sage Durvasa. He was the one who had come to her father's palace the spring before with the demand that he be served by one of royal blood. His booming voice, fuming eyes and filthy, weather-beaten body brooked no refusal. As always, King Kuntibhoja, feeble to the wills of saints and sages, whom he believed to have yogic powers and heavenly influence, had offered Kunti to Durvasa as his humble servant. He had ordered her to do as the great Sage demanded and refuse him nothing. Courtiers had stared and priests had blushed at this statement. Kunti had kept silent, downcast lids hid her scared eyes.

Now, facing, all alone, the consequence of her father's heartless words, Kunti felt utter hatred for him as she fumbled with the large bamboo basket in her hands. Inside, on a bundle of white sheets, lay a new-born boy, his wrinkled skin still stained with small patches of sticky blood. He slept soundly with eyes squeezed shut and hands balled into tiny fists. Fists that Kunti longed to coax open with gentle fingers, while cooing soft nothings into his ears. He was a beautiful baby, golden brown in complexion with a full head of soft, downy hair. His eyes were strikingly black, with the longest lashes she had ever seen in a baby. In his ears shone a pair of golden loops that Kunti's handmaiden had pierced just moments ago as Kunti slipped a pair of thick, golden bangles onto his wrists. An offering, they were, to the people she hoped would find him.

It was broad daylight and soon someone would stroll past. Still, Kunti looked upon her sleeping son, indulging herself for a few last moments. A short while back, he had been safe inside her swollen womb. She had hidden his presence carefully these last two seasons, staying within the secure walls of the women's wing after her saree could no longer conceal her distended belly. The physician, royal women and the eunuchs of the zenana had kept her secret well, telling her father and the court that she was bedridden, recovering from a mild bout of typhus.

Kunti wept uncontrollably when the other women suggested giving up her child when it was born. She was an unmarried princess, they said, a virgin according to the world outside. A bastard child would not only ruin her reputation forever but her father's as well. Kunti stayed silent. He was no father of hers. He deserved to be humiliated, punished for the callousness he had shown her whole life, she thought to herself. But choices were not a luxury she had with a belly that harboured seed from an ill-conceived, unwed union. Eventually, she agreed to give her child up, for there was little chance that the man she called father would allow her to keep it, if he found out. In fact, he would probably order the palace midwives to drown it in a bucket of cow's milk, the usual fate of unwanted babies.

This way, at least her son had a chance at life, Kunti thought. As she looked into his face, she wondered if she would ever see him again. And, if she did, would she recognise him? She bent to take a closer look at him, to commit to memory his features when she noticed that his bronze face now had a slight, pale tint of blue.

Her heart froze. Kunti's mind raced back to the many times she had heard the palace midwives talk about 'blue babies', a condition when a newborn child forgets to breathe and can die within minutes. What did they do, she thought frantically. She put her finger under his nose. He had, indeed, stopped breathing. 'You must suck the water from its nose and mouth and rub the chest until it starts to breathe,' she remembered an old hag instruct an apprentice midwife when it had happened to a handmaiden's child. Kunti had watched in awe as the woman had sucked at the child's face and roughly shoved at its chest while she spat a sticky fountain of yellow water onto the floor. The child had then screamed and gone from blue to pink and then red with fury at being awakened.

Kunti looked upon her son, now turning bluer, and she bent instinctively to repeat the midwife's ministrations. But before she could reach him, she stopped. 'His future is uncertain,' a voice inside her had whispered. 'He may be attacked by an animal when the river runs through the forest,' it said. No, she thought, shaking her head in horror, refusing to acknowledge such a gruesome possibility. 'He may be picked up by a beggar and made to live a life worse than death. He may become a slave, a leper, a criminal,' the voice continued relentlessly. Kunti cringed inside. He may live, be picked up by a noble woman, may even return to me someday, she weakly argued with the voice.

But it was persistent. 'Let him slip away now,' it whispered softly. 'He will feel no pain.'

Kunti's heart raced. Her sleeping child would be dead in a few minutes were she to do nothing. Yet, she stood still, surprising even herself. It was as if her body refused to do her mind's will, refused to do what she knew would be right. Seconds passed and the voice continued happily, 'yes, let him sleep. He would have been a black mark in your life.'

Kunti looked on, her breaths laboured, as the blue in his face became a little deeper.

'He would have hated you if he had lived.'

It spread to his tiny neck and shoulders.

'Why should you have to pay for that man's cruelty?'

Kunti blinked. Her hand flew to her son's chest as she bent and clamped his nose with her lips and sucked.

The man she called father would have ordered this baby executed, the moment he found out about it. He would have had no thought for it, just as he had no thought for her when he ordered her to serve the Sage Durvasa.

Kunti felt bitter stickiness in her mouth as she rubbed the baby's tiny chest, pushing at it frantically.

She was not like that man. She would never be like him.

She spat out the vile liquid and sucked at his tiny mouth. Tears flowed down the side of her face and on to her son. I'm sorry, she pleaded with him silently. Please live. You don't deserve to die because of him.

For a moment, he lay deathly still. Then, his lips twitched slightly under hers and she felt his tiny body cough. Kunti rubbed harder. She sucked out the last of the yellow water and spat it out just as she felt him inhale greedily. Her son would live. A cry emerged from his taut inside, a protest against her rough handling. It echoed loudly against the trees and she shushed him desperately in between her tears. They cried together for a few moments.

A loud thud in the distance caught Kunti's attention. The baby was wailing loudly. Too loudly not to be heard. Time was running out. The evening, with all its bustle, would soon be upon them.

She looked upon her son. She couldn't say goodbye. Instead, she held the basket tightly, hugging it. 'Oh, river mother!' she prayed silently, 'keep him alive and find him a good home, a loving mother. Let her be everything to him that I cannot.'

She squinted up at the sun, blazing and said softly, 'I give this child to you o' Surya, God of the Sun. From now on, he shall be your son. Look over him in my absence. Let him not suffer for he is blameless.' She closed her eyes as another sob racked her body, 'And please,' she whispered, 'let him not hate me for I had no choice.'

The river meandered gently, carefully past the palace gardens as the sun, glowing with the tenderness of twilight, looked upon the scene. There were few sounds to be heard in those moments apart from the wail of her baby. Yawning birds would soon flutter their eyes open after their nap, like the people, in the shade of the trees and sing their last song of the day, a lullaby she hoped would lull her baby to sleep in her absence. Yes, the world would stir soon and the convoluted humdrum of life would carry on as usual, reassuringly unchanged.

But, as she watched her precious cargo be taken by the river, to an unknown destiny, Princess Kunti knew she would never be the same again.

GANDHARI'S CONCLUSION

❦

She felt the pressure, numbing pressure, bearing down on her temples. Her breathing stalled, her muscles seized. She clutched her hair and fought against the darkness of fury, building whirlpool-like into a storm within her. She felt like screaming like an animal, like ripping her small tent out of the ground and thrashing it wildly against the trees in the forest, again and again, until this anger was spent.

She reached out and groped until she found her walking stick, a thin, carved bamboo pole plated with the finest gold, burnished and smooth, and inlaid with the reddest of rubies and corals. Red was her best colour, they had said. It suited her fine features and fair complexion, her long, black blanket of hair, her tall stature that dwarfed even some unfortunate men. Red was also the colour of her rage. She ground the rounded end of the walking stick into the toes of her naked feet, pressing harder and harder, gasping at the agonising pain it caused her. It will surely bleed this time, she thought distractedly as she squeezed her eyes shut and pressed again.

Slowly, the pressure subsided, the anger sinking to her feet, a mere throbbing pain now. She reached down and touched her toes. They were dry. A flutter of disappointment spread over her. It was almost as if a bloodied wound would have been an appropriate metaphor for what she felt, giving life to the rage that rampaged through her insides whenever it reared its snake-like head.

Her eyes were dry too, she discovered as she slipped a finger under the white, silken cloth that blindfolded her. This surprised Gandhari, former Queen of Hastinapur, less than the absence of a wound. She couldn't remember the last time she had cried. It was as if her eyes had given up more than just their sight when she had resolutely tied the cloth around them almost four decades ago.

Despite herself, her mind went back to that moment as she remembered the last thing she had ever seen. It had been early morning in Hastinapur and the slanted rays of the infant sun had woven playfully through the tree outside to cast a patterned, golden sheen upon the marble floor in her lavish bedchambers, decorated with sacred mango leaves, bridal marigolds and the reddest of flowers in her honour. Her jewelry, the old, which she had brought with her and the new, gifted yesterday on huge silver trays as she had arrived, lay scattered carelessly over the bed, divans and floor along with countless cloths and sarees of patterned, embellished silk. But their glitter and opulence was not what she remembered most about that morning. The morning sun's rays had also caught a copper basin filled with water, for washing her feet, which lay near the door, making it dazzle and glint as if it were made of an almost celestial metal. Gandhari remembered that glint bounce off her eyes as if it were yesterday. She had squinted as if confronted by the divine. She remembered her hands, soft, young and supple, stained with the auspicious red dye of brides. But most vividly of all, she remembered the horrified face of her chief handmaiden, Satvika, as she stood opposite Gandhari in her bedchambers. She had been crying and her kohl had run black trails down her hollow cheeks and sweaty lip. She had held her wrinkled hands folded together in a desperate plea for Gandhari to change her mind. Gandhari remembered the white, silken wash cloth she had held, carefully folded and then tied around her eyes, imprisoning them in darkness till this day.

She took her fingers out of the cloth, keeping her eyes firmly closed, so no light would enter them as her fingers disturbed the cloth. She had always done that, denied herself even the merest whisper of sight. Her experience of blindness had to be as complete as her husband, the former King of Hastinapur, Dhritarashtra's was.

A rustle outside her tent returned her to earthly concerns and the hot, dry stillness of the summer afternoon. She hoped it wasn't an animal foraging for food. They had precious little left after last week, when a group of monkeys had raided their three flimsy linen tents. The monkeys had not only wreaked havoc by thrashing fruit and herbs about and screaming at Dhritarashtra's attendant Sanjaya's weak attempts to stop them but had almost bitten her sister-in-law Queen-mother Kunti. Her husband would have to consider moving their camp-site if the raids kept up. With their condition as it was, weak from constant fasting, it would be a struggle too unbearable to imagine.

'Who is there?' she called out sharply in her most intimidating voice. Much to her relief, familiar footsteps, crackling over broken twigs and dried leaves, approached the tent and she heard the swish of her tent's linen opening being drawn aside. These tentative footsteps, tread by a flat, heavy foot in wooden slippers were careful to step softly, as if to walk with one's full weight was ill-mannered. The owner of these knew how sensitive Gandhari was to loud noises and had always done this to please her. Gandhari smiled with irony. In fact, the careful, hesitant treading had always irked her instead, but she had kept quiet over the decades to spare her husband's feelings.

'Do you smile, my wife?' said Dhritarashtra as he sat, with some difficulty, next to her on the forest floor.

Gandhari imagined an old, faceless man dressed in deerskin sitting on the rough earth, his bare legs, accustomed to silks and the finest linen, being dug into by sharp pebbles. Her smile grew milder, 'How do you always know when I smile, o' King?'

'I can hear it,' Dhritarashtra said simply.

Gandhari knew not what a smile sounded like. Her ears, constantly flooded with sounds, were obviously too inexperienced to hear it. Even after all these years, they were still learning how to be eyes. Today, amid the energetic swish of the trees against the hot, dry wind, called 'lu' in the dialect of these parts, and the singing of the birds and crickets, she had heard a new kind of frog croaking. It had sounded like someone saying, 'come in' again and again. She had laughed for the first time in months. That was before her thoughts had wandered and the rage had stormed into her serene moment.

Dhritarashtra began to speak but, instead, had a coughing fit.

Amidst the racking of his throat, Gandhari could hear the phlegm bubble in his chest and knew he was very sick. She also knew it was pointless to try and convince him to return to Hastinapur, where his nephew Yudhishthira was now king, to seek medical attention. Old men are supposed to be sick, Dhritarashtra would say. He had left Hastinapur for good, to end his days in fasting and spiritual contemplation in the forest. She knew from Sanjaya that her husband had become a little more than skin and bones these last months.

Her own fasting had become almost extreme and she could feel herself shrinking with every passing day as she ruthlessly scrubbed her body in the stream nearby. Kunti, who slept next to her in the tent, also seemed ravaged, her voice unsteadily weak and her sleep disturbed. Gandhari sighed. Often, she would be woken to hear Kunti mumbling incoherently in her sleep. 'No' she would say again and again, or 'Back, bring him back.' At these times Gandhari couldn't help but inwardly berate her sister-in-law's unwitting inconsideration. Kunti's five sons were alive and well, the rulers of Hastinapur. If anyone should be brought back it should be her own sons . . . Gandhari shook her head to clear it. Such thoughts would bear no fruit.

Dhritarashtra had now recovered from his coughing and said in a mild, raspy voice, 'You are disturbed? Was it something I said, my beautiful one?'

This tribute, given so often, never failed to inspire a playful, somewhat sarcastic retort from her. Today, her affectionate reply was stained with a hint of sadness, of bitterness, 'How can you be so sure that I'm beautiful o' King? You have never seen my face. You have had only the words of your servants and subjects to guide you.'

Dhritarashtra paused for a few long moments before shifting his position and replying in a steady way, 'I never needed others to tell me my wife is beautiful. I have felt it in the contours and smoothness of your person, witnessed it in the way you have conducted yourself as queen, heard it in your guidance and council, experienced it in your love for our children. I have told you this many times, yet you have never welcomed my compliments.'

Dhritarashtra paused and took a deep, rattling breath. Gandhari knew he was considering his next words and stayed silent, her heart beating quickly in anticipation. He spoke again, this time with a resigned tone, 'My days in this world will soon come to an end. I have not the time or patience to wait for you to forgive me, Gandhari. Yes, you were not told I was blind when our marriage was fixed. You were misled despicably and that is one of my life's biggest regrets. I was too young and too powerless to do anything about it at that time. Since then, I have spent a lifetime trying to make amends, give you my love and devotion. I have tried, Gandhari, I have tried ...,' his voice trailed into a deep sigh.

Gandhari played with the ends of her deerskin wrap and tried to focus her mind on the sound of their combined breathing and not the loud thumping of her heart. Dhritarashtra had never said these words to her, never acknowledged that she was tricked into marrying him by his Uncle Bhishma and her father. The night before her wedding it had been when white-faced Satvika had tearfully told her that her groom was blind from birth.

Dhritarashtra gathered his strength in a long breath before he continued, 'I had looked for support in my wife, someone through whom I could see the world. You could have been the light of my life, instead you became my partner in darkness. I have waited a lifetime for you to realise the foolishness, the cruelty of your decision and remove that cursed cloth from your eyes. The fact that you have not done so yet is testament to how much you truly hate me ...'

'I don't hate you,' Gandhari protested.

'... how much you still want to punish me and your family for what we did to you,' Dhritarashtra continued, unhindered. His hand scraped against the mud floor of the tent just as a loud gust of wind shook the linen folds of the tent in a dull thudding. Dhritarashtra was out of breath and obviously weak. The scraping grew louder as Gandhari heard him lay down and felt his head come to rest in her lap, his face upwards.

Despite herself Gandhari thought back to the first time that Dhritarashtra had lay down like this in her bedchamber on their wedding night. He had felt the cloth on her face and been amused. He had laughed as she had awkwardly stumbled about in confusion. Her husband had thought it a passing fancy that she should want to share his blindness and had not an inkling of the sheer panic and despair that had gripped his young, outwardly composed bride. The darkness had closed around her as if she were being buried alive, stifling her breathing, confounding her thoughts. It was from that endless well of despair that anger had emerged, a seething that focused her, kept her from losing her mind in the eternal night of her life. She had hugged this anger to herself as it grew slowly and ultimately into bouts of almost uncontrollable rage.

The wind and the thud of the tent ceased for a few moments. A bird, possibly a *koel*, sang with gusto just outside and she could hear the faint rustle of steps in the distance. Sanjaya had taken Kunti for a stroll earlier, to find the remains of a hermitage that stood in the area. Perhaps they were returning, or it was just a flock of deer grazing? Gandhari could not tell. Dhritarashtra was breathing deeply. She knew not what to say to him.

Her husband's voice, when it came, was almost a whisper, 'Forgive an old man, Gandhari and take off your cloth. We will reach the end of our lives soon. Punish me not so much that you will take away the pleasure of seeing this beautiful world in these last years from yourself. Forgive me.'

Gandhari was silent, too taken aback to respond. Then, slowly, tentatively, tears, actual tears, stung her eyes, bringing them to life for the first time since her wedding day. They tethered on the brink of her eyelid before being soaked up by the cloth. She put a finger to it and felt small, moist patches on the outside. She marvelled at the feeling just as loose drops of water began to flood her nostrils and a heaving overtook her chest. She sniffed and choked and hiccupped without being able to stop and noises, small moans, began to emanate involuntarily from her throat. The cloth around her eyes was much wetter now, her fingers told her. She squeezed her eyes shut but that only seemed to aggravate the flow of tears. She was crying, Gandhari realised in surprise. Elation, like never before, mingled with her tears and she gave up control, giving in to the bliss of release. She moaned loudly and sobbed, bending forward to rest her face on her husband's chest for comfort like a child while cradling his head in her arm like a mother.

Moments, minutes, eons passed and the anger of a lifetime slipped away with her tears onto her husband's chest. She wiped his drenched chest hair with her fingers and smiled with newfound freedom. She managed to say between her sobs, 'You are right, my husband. Forgive me, for I've only just realised what a spiteful fool I've been. No longer will I make you, or myself, wait.'

She sat up and pulled at the cursed cloth with shaking fingers. It came off and, as she threw it to the side, she felt a nervous pang in her stomach. Excitement pounded at her as she opened her eyes slowly.

Blackness. She felt around her head. Had she not moved the cloth? She felt her face, free from any obstruction. Her eyes, yes, they were open. She blinked and then once more. Blackness. She rubbed her eyes vigorously. Still, the familiar blackness.

'My husband, I can't see,' her voice trembled. She shook Dhritarashtra's head, still resting on her lap. It fell off with a thud onto the forest floor. She clutched at his face, his chest and shook harder, 'Help me! O' King, my husband. Why . . . Why aren't you helping me?' Dhritarashtra gave no response, his body was still and lifeless.

Gandhari froze. A chill, cold and merciless, gripped her heart tightly. With shaking fingers she felt for Dhritarashtra's face and placed her index finger under his nose. He wasn't breathing.

Gandhari screamed. A piercing un-human sound that caused the birds to flee from their trees with a loud flutter. She screamed till her voice ran hoarse. And then, something that had not happened in a long time began to happen to her.

The darkness started closing in.

Gandhari stood and fumbled with the flimsy tent until it collapsed on her. She managed to pry apart its entrance with her shaking fingers and bolted out, taking deep breaths. She felt the searing afternoon sun on her face and the dry, prickly forest floor jab into the soles of her feet. 'Kunti! Sanjaya!' she screamed again and again into the blackness as it began to slowly strangle her. Her voice bounced off the trees and echoed into the distance and droplets of sweat bathed her person. She clutched her throat and ran, where she knew not. All she knew was, she had to get away from the blackness, for it was no longer a friend, an accomplice in her revenge against the world. It was now a predator, clutching at her windpipe, waiting for her struggle to end, so it could choke her to death.

Her voice was a hysterical sob as she called, 'Kunti! Sanjaya!' before she tripped violently over a pile of debris so hot that it burned her soles. She fell with a scream of pain, thrashing her feet and sending the debris flying away from her. Ashes, she realised as she sat up and clutched her burned feet. Sanjaya had lit a fire last night. He had said there was talk of a tiger in the area and didn't want to take any chances. Gandhari remembered distractedly her husband warn Sanjaya to put the fire out properly in the morning as it was the dry season and forest fires were quite common. Suddenly, her right ankle erupted, shooting painful spasms up her leg as she tried to move it. Overcome with fear and panic, her ankle and feet throbbing in agony, Gandhari wailed and collapsed on to the forest floor.

As she slipped out of consciousness, Gandhari absently wondered if a person could die from blindness, a broken ankle and regret.

As she awoke in her dream, she saw the copper basin, shimmering in the morning sunlight, and from it magically emerged her mother, dressed in a white widow's saree. Her mother's compassionate eyes caressed her but she said nothing. Gandhari could feel her warmth as they stood facing each other for what seemed like eternity. She stepped forward to hug her, to lay her face in her mother's breast and weep like a child once more when she felt something shaking her vehemently.

The dream, so full of light, slipped away and Gandhari awoke to the darkness once again. This time, she felt calm. Her ankle still throbbed, but the pain in the burnt soles of her feet had almost gone, leaving behind only a numb sensation. What she did feel, quite distinctly, was the acrid smell of smoke flood her nostrils. She also felt heat, intense heat all around her as she heard Kunti's voice say, 'Sister! Wake up. We must hurry.'

Gandhari's voice was a soft groan, 'Sister Kunti. Thank god you are here.' She coughed to let the smoke out of her throat.

Kunti's voice was full of anguish, 'Sister Gandhari, open your eyes and get up, we must leave.'

Gandhari was dimly aware of a crackling sound around them but the pain of her fall made it hard to concentrate.

She said with a wry shudder, 'There is no point in opening my eyes, o' sister. I am blind. And, my husband is dead. I have been punished.'

Kunti caught hold of her shoulder, 'Sanjaya has found him, sister and performed his last rites. But we must leave. The forest is on fire!'

Gandhari snapped to her senses. Suddenly, she realised the smoky stench was of burning wood and foliage. She felt the waves of heat wash over her and hear the crackling, louder with each passing moment. The fire from last night . . . she had tripped over it. She returned Kunti's desperate grip, 'I fell over and scattered last night's embers, sister. I think that might be what caused it. Can we not thrash it out?'

Kunti squeezed her shoulder, 'It is spreading too fast sister. Two trees have already started burning and the grass is aflame as well. We must escape quickly. We will have to leave the king behind.'

Gandhari was quiet for a moment and then said, 'No. I cannot. My ankle is broken.'

Kunti called out to Sanjaya and then said, 'Sanjaya will carry you, sister.'

Gandhari shook her head, 'It will be too much for him. He is weak from fasting. I will stay here, Kunti.' She heard Sanjaya's footsteps run up to her.

'My queen, are you hurt?' his young voice was shaking and teary.

Gandhari lifted her hand, felt his face and wiped away the tears. She said softly, 'You were more than just his eyes. He loved you like a son.'

Sanjaya cried harder, his body heaving, but said through his tears, 'We must escape this fire, o' queen. You must stand up.'

Gandhari smiled sadly, 'I cannot stand Sanjaya. My ankle is broken and so is my resolve. My husband is dead. I will stay here and go with him.'

Sanjaya was vehement, 'I will carry you, o' queen . . .'

'No,' Gandhari said softly, 'You must go and take Kunti with you.'

For a moment neither Sanjaya nor Kunti spoke. Then Kunti said, 'I will stay with you.'

Gandhari said, 'No,' but Kunti interrupted, 'Please. What can I hope to achieve now by staying alive? I am old like you, sister and, like you, I am tired. I will stay.'

Gandhari nodded and took a deep breath.

Sanjaya cried desperately, 'Please I beg of you both. Let me help you to safety. My king would have wished it.'

Gandhari replied, 'You are a young man, Sanjaya. You must leave now. This is the wish of your queen.'

Kunti spoke to Sanjaya, 'Go now my child. Go quickly,' and after a moment, 'I command you to leave.'

Sanjaya sobbed but got to his feet slowly. Gandhari felt him touch her feet gently and then, he was gone. She sighed and said, 'You will stay?'

Kunti replied softly, 'I will.'

Gandhari propped herself up weakly, 'Then, help me to sit up, my sister.'

She managed to sit up with Kunti's help. Her ankle hurt relentlessly but she was past caring. It would be over soon.

Kunti slipped her hand under hers, 'You are blind, sister?'

'Yes.'

A moment's silence.

Kunti said, 'He loved you.'

Gandhari whispered, 'And I, him.'

The heat was almost unbearable now. Her nostrils flooded with stinging smoke and she could hear loud snaps and crashes all around as branches fell burning from the trees. Gandhari held Kunti's hand and began to pray. Soon, her nostrils choked and her head swam. She coughed a few times before losing consciousness.

BHISHMA'S TEMPTATION

❧

𝔅hishma sighed. On the far right of the court, a few courtiers had the audacity to chuckle. He looked over at them and glared. They cowed immediately, their eyes falling sheepishly to the brilliant marble floor.

Bhishma knew not what to say and sighed again, this time with impatience, at his own inarticulacy. His eyes fell on the scene before him. The royal court of Hastinapur, in all its gilded glory, stretched out layer by layer into what seemed like a considerable distance. Flanking both sides the throne on which he sat as regent for his underage half-brother King Vichitravirya, were the hundred or so royal courtiers, all men, seated on raised, cushioned platforms. The eldest of these sat the closest to him as a mark of greater distinction. Interspersed with the courtiers were the few visiting sages and royals, the more important of which sat closer to the throne. Behind the courtiers, along the centre aisles, sat the priests of the kingdom, on silken floor cushions. Behind them, in a large covered yard with a stone floor, were those of the warrior and noble class and then those of the merchant class. At the very end of the court, on the muddy ground in the open air, sat the men and women of the villages, the farmers and the unfortunate poor on woven mats. Of course, the true unfortunates, the untouchable caste of servants, undertakers and beggars were outside the royal court gates, tucked away out of sight in a queue, awaiting the regent's charity. Bhishma's eyes fell on his royal guards with their bright red turbans. They stood in a line along the entire perimeter of the crowd, armed with swords and long sticks with sharpened edges that were slung criss-crossed on their bare backs with horse hide. And then, Bhishma's eyes returned to where they were earlier. Right in front of him in the centre aisle, stood one of the most beautiful women he had ever seen.

Her face was covered by a red gossamer veil that did little to hide the brilliance of her light brown eyes, the soft sheen of her olive skin or the natural pout of her heart-shaped lips. Her nose was quite regal, thought Bhishma absently, pert and straight under the tinkling gold ring that hung from it. Her red saree, simply yet elegantly decorated with golden paisley hugged the equally elegant curves on her body. She was not voluptuous, like many royal women who enjoyed their fair share of sweetmeats. Instead, her curves were ... just right, thought Bhishma, for a discerning man who had moderate tastes.

A fidget from her brought Bhishma's thoughts screaming into the present. He stiffened as he realised what he had been doing. A chaste man must never succumb to unchaste thoughts, he told himself before considering his next words.

'Princess Amba,' he said steadily to the woman who stood before him, 'as the world knows, I took a vow of chastity when I was an adolescent to ensure that my stepbrother and his kin inherit the throne of Hastinapur. Hence, it is quite impossible for me to marry you.'

Princess Amba's expression was muted by the veil to all else but Bhishma, sitting as he was directly in front of her, saw the angry flash in her eyes as she responded, 'All I know is that I was, along with my sisters, abducted by you at my *swayamwara.*

As my abductor, it falls upon you to take charge of my destiny.' She looked up at him, 'I am your responsibility.'

Bhishma grew impatient. This princess, beautiful as she may be, had been nothing but a nuisance since they met. Agreed, he had forcibly kidnapped her from her *swayamwara* and brought her to Hastinapur with her two sisters, but that had been, so the three could marry his stepbrother Vichitravirya. Despite being in the prime of his life, he had no intention of marrying them himself. He recalled that Amba had been the one to resist the hardest and had wept miserably in the carriage as they made their way to Hastinapur. He had found out why only when they arrived. She was in love with King Salwa of Saubala and she would have chosen him as her husband at the Swayamwara had Bhishma not abducted her first. Upon hearing this, Vichitravirya refused to marry her. Bhishma had then given orders for her to be taken to the kingdom of Saubala so she could be taken by Salwa as his bride. But, upon her arrival, Salwa had refused to marry her. He had told her that, having been taken at the *swayamwara* by another man, she could not be his wife. She was Bhishma's property, he said, and should go back to Hastinapur and marry him instead.

Bhishma sighed for the third time as he looked upon the princess. To send her back to her father's kingdom would be the ultimate rejection and she would be a social outcaste, a widow without even a husband's name. Marrying her was out of the question, of course. His vow was sacred and he would rather end his own life than break his word. What was he to do with her, he wondered.

He cleared his throat and said, 'You have spent much of the winter journeying between kingdoms and must be tired. Perhaps, it would be best if you were to remain in Hastinapur as our guest until you decide a course for your life. I'm sure you will enjoy the time spent with your sisters.'

Amba responded with sarcasm at his patronising tone, 'Am I to spend the rest of my life being your guest? I am a princess and it is my dharmic duty to marry. An unmarried woman is either a sage, a servant of god, a prostitute or as good as dead.'

Bhishma repeated firmly, 'I cannot marry you, Princess Amba, and that is final.'

Amba's tone was barely civil, 'You took ownership of my person but do not give me your name. Is this morally correct for a great man as yourself, o' Bhishma?'

Bhishma had had enough. To be challenged by a mere woman in court was unacceptable. He waved to a courtier, 'Take Princess Amba to the women's quarters and request her sisters, the queens Ambika and Ambalika, to make sure she is comfortable.'

A courtier waved Amba away as Bhishma resolutely turned his attention to the next matter on the court's agenda.

Twenty-one moons passed before Bhishma laid eyes on Amba again. It was a glorious, spring day and the kingdom was celebrating Holi, the festival of colour and feasting. The weather was dry and cool, the birds sang robustly and all the trees were draped in coy buds of spring flowers. The muddy streets of Hastinapur were covered in pools of water stained red and yellow from the vermillion and turmeric that dripped from laughing faces. Adolescent boys grinned gleefully as they rubbed each other with the coloured powder and ran for cover after throwing pots of water on their friends. Older men sat back under trees, looking quite comical with their red and yellow faces, and drank sweet milk mixed with *bhang*, a locally grown opiate. Women giggled and screamed loudly as they chewed the *bhang* leaf and drenched each other with colour in the privacy of courtyards and then ran to windows to watch the scene on the streets. Later, when everyone had cleansed themselves of all proof of the day's wantonness and the temporary insanity implanted by the *bhang* had worn off, there would be prayer and then the feasting.

Bhishma was offered the heady milk mixture but declined. He didn't like anything interfering with his self-control and *bhang* was known to be a strong aphrodisiac. He sat on a silken divan in the royal gardens with the elders and watched indulgently while the courtiers, children of the royal ladies and their servants played Holi before him. Once every so often, a child would approach him tentatively and rub a small amount of vermillion or turmeric on his cheek with a finger. Bhishma would smile and lean forward when they approached but even the children knew better than to invite him to play with them.

He looked around and appreciated the artistry of the royal gardeners. The ponds, with their fat resident geese, were bursting with pink lotuses in half-bloom, marigold flowers dotted the landscape right up till the horizon. The scent of black aloe hung huskily in the air. Bhishma took a deep breath and let himself take in the sensual vigour of spring time.

Suddenly, in the distance on his far right, he caught a movement in the bushes. The warrior in him awoke as he focused on the rustling. His trained eye saw a flash of white clothing and then the bush was still.

Bhishma looked around. Everybody seemed to be wholly engrossed in the festivities. He felt the gold hilt of the sword straddling his waist with his fingertips and got up gingerly. The rustling bushes were near the women's quarters, an area out of bounds for any man. Normally, the rules were never flouted but

Bhishma would not have been surprised to encounter a young courtier under the influence of *bhang* spying on the women playing Holi. He strode purposefully towards the offending plant, bracing himself to deliver a scathing speech and perhaps a sword graze or two, to the culprit behind it.

When he got there, however, he was taken completely by surprise. Lying unconscious in the bushes was a woman. She lay on her stomach, face down, her white saree soaking wet and copiously stained with red vermillion.

Bhishma bent quickly and turned her around onto her back. Her long wet hair slapped against his wrist as he held the back of her head and looked into her face for signs of breathing. It was Princess Amba. He put a finger under her nose. She was breathing but it was shallow and her body shivered slightly.

Bhishma looked towards the women's quarters but there was nobody in plain sight. He would have to take her in and hand her over to the hags, who administered to the royal women. He put one around her back and the other under her knees and lifted her limp body easily. He then strode through the gardens and into the women's quarters.

Unlike his elders and half-brother, who routinely visited royal wives in their chambers, Bhishma had never been inside the women's wing before. His vow of chastity had sealed off that side of the palace to him for life. Now, he wandered blindly around the passageways looking for a female face. It was completely deserted. He yelled loudly, 'Is anyone here? Come out! Princess Amba needs help.' But he got no reply.

Bhishma exclaimed in exasperation and looked down at his charge. Her eyes were closed, her lips parted in a swoon as her head hung back. Her long, wet hair fanned over his arm and almost touched the floor. Her body still shivered.

He walked around in the courtyard until he saw a door ajar and kicked it open. Inside, was a dark bedchamber with a small window on the side, obviously belonging to a female of lower rank. The sun's rays peeped through to reveal a large, divan-like wooden bed in the centre of the room, sparsely covered with white cotton bedclothes. Apart from a large iron trunk and an earthen water pot with a copper cup near the door, the room had little else in it.

Bhishma lay Amba down on the bed and hurriedly poured some water from the pot. He then splashed some onto her face and shook her roughly saying,

'Princess, wake up.'

Amba groaned and pulled her face away from his voice. Her back arched as if in pain. Her saree, still drenched with coloured water, clung to her body and Bhishma found himself unable to avoid looking at her. Her breasts heaved against the thin, translucent, cloth that bound them, their dark, erect nipples clearly visible. Droplets of water ran slowly, one by one, down the length of her arched neck onto smooth, naked shoulders. Bhishma's eyes travelled to her uncovered navel, normally demurely tucked away in the folds of her saree, now twisting sinuously as she awoke. He drew a sharp breath and tried to master his arousal.

Amba opened her eyes and looked at Bhishma in a surprised daze. Her breath shivered as she took in air. She said in a soft whimper, 'Bhishma?'

His pulse throbbed and thighs contracted. Bhishma's entire body ached with alien feelings that he thought he had long ago overcome. Women had tried to seduce him ever since his voice lost its childish lilt and his body discarded chubby smoothness for the rough muscularity of warriors. They had tried every true trick known to womankind, but Bhishma had never been moved enough to succumb. Yet, looking at this woman now, unadorned and vulnerable, laying in front of him drenched and covered in red vermillion, he just wanted to, to . . .

'I . . . I must have fainted. Where am I?' Amba said softly as she stirred and slowly sat up on the bed, completely unaware of the reason behind the taut look on Bhishma's face.

Bhishma knew he should stand up and put some distance between them but he couldn't bring himself to move. His voice was thick when he replied, 'I found you in the gardens. You're in the women's wing.'

Amba's eyes widened as she noticed the hoarseness of his tone, the rigid closeness of his body. He radiated warmth from the shallow breaths that entered and left his craggy face, with its well-oiled and neat mustache and weather-beaten eyes. Disoriented though she was, it was difficult not to see the plain look of desire in Bhishma's face and not read the obvious arousal of his body. The woman in her, inexperienced but articulate in the ways of love, instinctively recognised the power she had over him in this delicate moment. She smiled.

Bhishma, master of many a retreating army, had never fought a war as treacherous as the one he now fought with himself. He willed himself not to stare at her supple body, bursting from its flimsy, drenched confines. He wanted to smear the red vermillion powder on her neck and shoulders all over her body with his hands. He wanted to wind the long, wet strands of her thick hair in his fist and pull her head back so he could kiss her perfect, little lips and the smooth arch of her throat. He wanted to pull that god-forsaken piece of cloth from her body and see her nakedness in all its glory.

Amba's eyes were now no longer foggy as she stared back at him. Her lips tilted in a knowing smile and she looked at him from behind her lashes coquettishly. Her voice was husky when she said, 'The women went to the river to play holi. The sun was too hot for me so I decided to come back. I must have been overcome before I reached my chambers,' she moved her face a little closer to his and whispered, 'Thank you for being my saviour, o' great Bhishma.' She lifted her hand to his cheek and brushed it with the lightest of touches.

Her touch sent a bolt through his body and he shuddered unwillingly. It was too much to bear. Bhishma caught hold of her wrist as it pulled away from his face and placed it back on his cheek. Then, he kissed it. He looked back at her, searching for a reaction.

Amba caressed his cheek with her fingers. She said nothing. She didn't need to.

Bhishma kissed her forearm and elbow before making his way towards her shoulders. His chest pounded and throbbed with each kiss as he felt the smoothness of her skin and tasted the bitter twang of the vermillion colour on it. He buried his face in her neck and ran his hands around her waist to pull her closer to him. Amba moaned softly, almost melodiously, and his hands became more urgent as they explored the curves of her navel and worked their way towards her breast. He kissed her neck, her chin and then her mouth, which trembled and moved under his insistence, sending waves of pleasure down his body.

Amba watched Bhishma closely through half-lidded eyes. She reached back and pulled open the knot that bound the cloth to her breasts just as Bhishma's hands reached them. He cupped and squeezed, his body shuddering as she moaned under his lips. She pulled him closer until their bodies touched and ran her hands in between the thick hairs on his chest and down his back.

Bhishma pushed Amba onto her back and lay on her side as he kissed her shoulders, breasts and navel. Then, when he grew impatient, he returned to her lips while his hands tugged softly at the saree which sat beneath her belly, trying to undo the folds.

Amba's eyes, unseen by Bhishma's closed ones, opened in panic. For a moment they were scattered, looking around in indecision. Then, she laughed softly, breathlessly as she felt Bhishma put his weight on her and his insistent hands pulled harder at her saree. She turned her face and whispered in his ear, 'Patience, my love,' said she, 'we have the rest of our lives. I promise I will not make you wait after our wedding.'

Bhishma's head snapped back and reeled as if he had just been plunged into the winter river. Wedding? He thought for a dazed moment. Then, a dizzying fear and mortification gripped his body. What was he doing? He stared into Amba's coy face with a horrified look on his own. Then, as fast as his body would allow, he pushed himself away and scrambled to his feet beside the bed.

'No,' Amba shouted as she reached out to Bhishma but then stopped as she saw the look on his face. For a moment, it seemed like she would burst into tears but then a steely resolve slowly emerged in her eyes and she spoke, 'You have taken advantage of me.'

Bhishma felt shame and guilt wash over him and seep into every pore in his body. He could not look into her accusing eyes. 'Forgive me, Princess,' he said as if in pain, 'I have wronged you.' My vow, he thought to himself. How could have I done this, almost committed the most heinous sin of all; broken my word, my dharma? He chastised himself severely, what face could I have shown to the gods had I committed this sinful act? He shook his head in sorrow and turned to leave the room.

'Where do you go? Will you leave me here like a serving girl, tarnished by your affections?' Amba taunted his retreating back.

Bhishma turned and faced her, still avoiding her eye, 'I have apologised for my actions, Princess. Beyond that, I can only assure you that you will never be subjected to this again.'

'That is not good enough,' Amba was sitting now, covering her breasts with her saree.

Bhishma was almost preoccupied when he replied, 'What is it you want? What can I give you that will show you how much I regret this?'

Amba's eyes momentarily flickered with hurt as he spoke but they remained hard and uncompromising, 'I want marriage. You have used me and my body. Who will accept a woman like me once I have been in your company in this way? You must do right by me. You must marry me.'

Bhishma, as yet unrecovered and incredulous at his own behaviour, was impatient and angry, 'I have told you woman, I cannot marry you. The gods know my vow, kept true till this day. I almost did the unthinkable today.'

'Your vow?' Amba stood up slowly, clutching the bed in a desperate way, 'From the moment you kidnapped me at my *swayamwara*, you have made me useless to any respectable man. I was one of the most desired princess in all the kingdoms and now I am a social pariah. Because of you o' great Bhishma. And all you think of is your vow? Damn your vow to hell. What about me?' she screamed.

Bhishma was shocked. He stared at her as if he couldn't believe she was capable of such words. Damn his vow? Obviously a mere woman could not comprehend the magnitude of a broken word or the importance of dharma. It was useless to try and explain it to her, he decided. He turned his attention, instead, on delicately extricating himself from this uneasy situation, 'A man cannot be blamed for his obligations princess. You are welcome to stay here as our guest for as long as you wish. Forever, if that is what you choose. I shall see to it that you are treated well and live comfortably.'

Amba's eyes burned with hate and anger, 'Live here as a guest,' she repeated, 'A guest without a home is as good as a beggar. I want a home, children, family.' She paused for an instant and then continued, 'I will not touch a grain of salt in your palace if you refuse to honour me.'

Bhishma turned his back to leave as he said, 'That is your wish princess.' He started to walk toward the door.

Amba called after him, 'No! You cannot leave like this.'

Bhishma answered without looking back, 'I have said all that is necessary.'

Amba ran and stood in front of him. Her eyes were desperate, her breaths short, 'Please, o' Bhishma. Please, I beg you. Do not do this.' She then kneeled and caught his ankle in her hands, her long hair sweeping the floor and her eyes brimming with tears as she looked up at him, 'I beg you, o' prince. Think of my life and future. Have mercy on me, please. I beg you. I beg for your charity, o' Bhishma.' Tears began to flow uncontrollably down her cheeks.

Bhishma didn't look down at her weeping face. Instead, he took a step back until his ankle was freed from her grasp and continued to the door.

For a moment, Amba sat silent, weeping and crumpled like a ragged doll on the floor. Then, her tears stopped and she looked up, her eyes hard and her expression contorted with hatred. Her voice rang clear and potent with unmasked fury, 'You have ruined my life, Bhishma. I will have my vengeance.' She got up and blocked his path at the door, a small but poisonous viper, spitting venom at the larger bull, 'I will kill you for what you have done to me. Do you hear me?'

Bhishma's arm brushed her aside and then pulled back as if scorched by her touch. He left briskly, his eyes unwaveringly ahead, his mind focused on the deep meditation he would need to do once he reached his chambers.

Amba looked at him walk away and clutched the folds of her saree closer to her bosom as she whispered once more to his retreating back, 'One day, I will kill you.'

KARNA'S DECEPTION

❦

𝔗he sun seemed to burn through the trees, forming millions of tiny, blazing circles of heat on the forest floor, smothered indiscriminately with weeds, fallen wild flowers, berries and branches and grizzly bushes at the base of huge, virgin tree trunks. The damp smell of growing life was partnered with the intensely sweet fragrance of wildflowers and the spicy muskiness of rotting forest berries.

Karna looked up and squinted as rays of sunlight flashed through his bushy eyelashes. His adoptive mother always said that he had the longest eyelashes she had ever seen on any man or woman. The rest of his face was craggy at best, lined and weathered despite being in the prime of life. His mouth had a natural downturn that people often mistook for a sour persona, but those close to Karna knew him to be quite the opposite. His philanthropic deeds were well known throughout Hastinapur, where he now lived with his best friend and adopted brother, Duryodhana. Of course how he could, the recipients of his charity and goodwill often commented, call a callous man like Duryodhana his friend was beyond their understanding. Karna was known to be everything his friend was not; good humoured, just and, above all, dharmic.

I should find a camp-site soon, Karna thought to himself as he egged his horse faster along the forest path with a flick of his ankle. The sun burned the brightest just before it mellowed and retired into the night. He had been riding hard since daybreak with only a short break in a forest hermitage. His horse Kali, named so not only because she was black as the desert night but because she was as ferocious in battle as the goddess of destruction, Kali herself, could probably go on until after sun down but he didn't want to risk tiring her. A hermitage would be the best place to spend the night, as they usually had provisions for animals, but if one didn't show itself in the near distance, he would just as easily set up a camp-site under the shade of a banyan tree and let Kali graze all night.

He looked down upon the back of his horse's head, and noticed her ears twitching, listening to the sound of his breathing. He stroked her neck and felt it quiver in response. He had never needed to tie her to a tree like other horses. She would never stray too far from him. The only female in this mortal realm truly devoted to me, he thought with a sardonic smile. Then, he remembered his adoptive mother Radha and corrected himself as his smile turned into one of genuine affection. From the moment his adoptive father Adhiratha the charioteer, had picked Karna, a new bornbaby in a basket, from the banks of the river Ganga and placed him in the hands of his wife, she had been utterly devoted to him.

As Karna looked around the forest path for signs of a hermitage, he allowed his thoughts to wander back to the place he had left yesterday. Hastinapur and the royal palace of Duryodhana's blind father, King Dhritarashtra, had been in turmoil for the last year as spies were sent throughout the kingdoms to look for the Pandava brothers and their common wife Draupadi. It was the last year of their thirteen-year exile and, as per the rules of the exile period, this year they had to remain incognito. Were they seen or recognised by anyone, another fourteen years in exile would follow.

Karna had little hope that they would be found for they were extremely intelligent and trained in the art of camouflage, an integral skill of the warrior. He had told Duryodhana this only to be met with his friend's legendary temper. 'They must be somewhere!' Duryodhana had exclaimed. He had begged Karna, his best friend and right-hand man, to go and find them.

Karna had always found it hard to deny Duryodhana, such was the debt he owed to his friend. Duryodhana had not only adopted Karna, a mere charioteer's son, as his brother but had even given him a small principality to rule over as a mark of his affection, elevating Karna's status from a servant to that of royalty. Karna knew Duryodhana was secretly scared of the Pandavas and didn't want to face them in battle after sending them into exile for so many years. So, with a reluctant heart, he had set out on the pretext of finding the Pandavas, uneasily telling Duryodhana that he would do his bit to ensure they went back into exile at the end of the year.

Karna fidgeted on Kali's back. He had never felt comfortable with the idea of exile or that game of dice almost thirteen years ago that had decided everything. He had long suspected that Duryodhana's uncle Shakuni had used questionable means to win. But he wasn't sure and Duryodhana had assured him that no foul play had occurred. Still, Karna's unease and the smallest pinch of guilt had stayed. He would have much preferred to defeat the Pandavas on the battlefield, with honour.

The shade of the trees slowly began to cool and a lonely cricket began to chirrup loudly, breaking Karna's reverie. It would be twilight soon, when the sun would burst into burnished turmeric radiance before it retired into the night. Shelter would have to be found soon.

Karna noticed a few, small threads of smoke against the horizon. Possibly, a hermitage or a nomadic settlement, he thought. It was some distance away but Karna was certain he could be there before the sun set. He hoped it was a tribe of nomads. A night spent among common folk who knew not his name and status would be welcome. His mouth watered at the thought of having a poor man's dinner tonight; *tharra*, a strong brew made from fermented wheat husk with a hearty mix of cooked lentils and onions fried in mustard oil with chillis along with large, thick *rotis* roasted over an open fire until their outsides blackened and became crusty but the insides remained soft and raw. Not for him were the delicate curries topped with almonds and thin, puffy *rotis* with cardamom scented clarified butter he was served at the palace. He may be a royal now, but his stomach was still as common as ever, he thought with a chuckle.

The settlement now became visible in the distance. It was a hermitage, Karna noted with an inadvertent twinge of disappointment. In the next instant he reprimanded himself. There may be no *tharra* for me tonight, he thought, but it is a privilege to spend an evening with learned men and I should consider myself blessed. He rode towards the hermitage resolutely.

Soon, he stood on his feet outside the earthen wall that separated the hermitage from the forest and rattled the wooden gate gently. He knew it was unlocked and he would be welcome, but courtesy demanded he be invited in for the night. An apprentice, a young boy of about thirteen summers with a shaven head, a white cloth around his waist and a sacred thread tied around his chest, came running to the gate. He gawped when he saw Karna standing outside in royal regalia with a war horse but had the wit to bow deeply with folded hands and open the gate. Karna entered the large courtyard and returned the greeting by placing his hand on the boy's head and blessing him. He smiled saying, 'Kali here is tired,' he gestured towards an old banyan tree in one corner of the courtyard, 'I'm sure she can be made comfortable over there with some grass to eat and water to drink.'

The apprentice looked almost scared of the big, black horse as he nodded and took the reins. Karna gave Kali's neck a last touch, put his slippers beside the gate and walked on barefoot through a large wooden door, towards the inner courtyard of the hermitage. This was a large open space with an earthen floor, at the centre of which stood a banyan tree as ancient as the forest itself. Its branches stretched outwards assertively, until they hung, almost tree-like, over gigantic roots that protruded out of the earth. An earthen ring had been constructed around the base of this tree, upon which lay a straw mat. More straw mats lay below, at the foot of the base, piled neatly in a stack.

Looking upon such a familiar scene reminded Karna of the days he had spent as an apprentice at a hermitage much like this one, except that it had been on the outskirts of Hastinapur, so he had been able to go on living at home and helping his father with his stable duties. Most of his clan, those of royal servants, didn't bother to send their children to sages to learn for they were considered more productive working from an early age, but his parents had always thought there was something distinctly noble about their adopted son and so they had sent him for a few hours a day. Every morning, after washing and prayer, Karna recalled, he would take a straw mat from a pile and sit on the ground while his teacher, an old, learned sage, would talk about life and dharma. The sons of noblemen and royalty were taught history, astronomy and mathematics but the rest of the boys had mostly been taught stories about the gods with important lessons about life at the end of them. Karna's favourite subject had been warfare and sport. Wrestling and mock sword fighting were often used by teachers as a means to vent the ample energy of young boys.

Karna looked around at the small mud huts distributed along the perimeter of the hermitage courtyard. The biggest one closest to the entrance, he knew, would house the apprentices. Then, there was the large hut with an attached shed where food was prepared, stocked and eaten, a hut where travelling sages and visitors slept and finally, a small hut in the corner belonging to the sage who was the head of the hermitage. He was obviously unmarried or a widower, Karna thought after noting its size. Sages with families usually lived in bigger huts at a distance from the rest, so their wives and daughters could have privacy.

Towards the back of the courtyard, behind the huts, was an enclosure at the centre of which was a small fire. This was the gathering place where prayers and rituals were conducted in the morning and meetings were held in the evening. There were twelve people sitting around the fire, Karna noted as he walked towards them. Eight were apprentices, the youngest of which must have seen only five summers, dressed in their white loincloths and sacred strings, sitting on one side. Two were obviously travelling mystics as could be told from their sun-scorched skin, grizzly appearance and deerskin attire. The head of the hermitage, an old, balding sage with a white beard sat quietly on another side, his bright, intelligent, yet kindly eyes contemplating the fire in deep thought. Next to him, diligently fanning the fire with a stick, was a younger man of around thirty summers. Probably, a distant relative who would take over the hermitage some day, Karna thought.

He approached the head sage and bowed low, his hands folded in supplication. He touched the sage's feet with both hands and then his own forehead, as a mark of respect. The sage acknowledged him with a brief, distracted but kindly, nod. Karna sat down on the ground next to him and looked into the fire. There would be no hurry to speak, he knew. Hermitages were places of quiet contemplation, especially in the evenings.

It was the time of twilight and Karna noticed a slight chill begin to creep into the air. It was always like this in these parts. The nights were as mild and cool as the days were hot. He was glad for the fire, not only as a source of light in what would soon be a black forest night, but also for its comforting warmth.

After a few moments, the head sage quietly spoke to the young man next to him, 'Our guest will be hungry.'

The man nodded and folded his hands as he got up and went to the hut where food was prepared. He returned a few minutes later and stood in the corner with a pot of water and a small cloth in his hands. Karna got up, gratefully washed and dried his hands, thanked the man with folded hands and returned to his seat. Another apprentice then appeared with a copper plate and set it in front of him. Boiled lentils, an assortment of fruit and nuts and some wild rice. Not the spicy, lustful meal he had hoped for, but his rumbling insides were grateful for it.

From the corner of his eye, Karna observed the others as he ate. The younger apprentices were fidgety, bored of the forced contemplative mood. The older ones sat still like stretched bowstrings, all restrained energy. Karna thought wryly, remembering his own experiences, that their energy would probably be spent when they went on their secret jaunt into the forest tonight. The mystics scrutinised him, his silken tunic, precious jewelry and golden amulets bearing his insignia curiously with their bright eyes. They would know him to be a royal, he was sure, for their kind regularly left the mountains and forests and ventured forth into towns to beg for alms, perform magical cures for a fee, buy favours from prostitutes and gather gossip about the local royals, which they could then circulate in other towns. Karna himself was quite contemptuous of their kind, being a staunch follower of Dharma. He knew they were usually flexible with their morals and often used magic and mysticism as a mask for some of their more questionable activities. It was not uncommon for a village family to find their teenage daughter with child after she had been 'cured' of an ailment by a travelling mystic.

The head of the hermitage looked up the fire in deep thought and respectfully said nothing until Karna had finished the last morsel on his plate and washed his hands. Then, he turned to his opulent visitor and said quietly, 'In which direction do you head, child?'

Karna smiled. No one called him a child these days. Not even his parents. He bowed his head, 'In whichever direction the wind takes me for the moment.' Then, he felt apologetic for being evasive with the kindly old man and so he added, 'I am from Hastinapur, o' respected sage. An aid of the king Dhritarashtra.'

' 'Indeed. I met King Dhritarashtra many moons ago, when he was a younger man. How is his health?'

Karna replied solicitously, 'Not as good as it used to be, but he is still quick of mind and strong of heart.'

The sage nodded and fell silent. After a few moments, he said, 'So the wind has brought you to our forest,' he said gently.

A question, Karna recognised, without the actual asking. It was quite common for riders to stay overnight at hermitages when they were on a king's mission, but Karna knew that royals, like he obviously was, usually travelled in groups with large entourages. So, it was no wonder the old man was curious as to what he was doing in deep forest without even an attendant. He decided to answer the question truthfully, yet give nothing away, 'I'm looking for something the king has lost.'

The old sage's eyes were quite detached when he asked, 'Why do you want to find it?'

Karna replied, 'Because it will please the king.'

The sage regarded him with gently eyes, 'Will it please you?'

Karna was quiet for a few moments as he considered his answer. Then, he said slowly, 'It will please the king and so it must please me.'

The old sage looked into his eyes for a moment and then fell silent once more.

One of the mystics, a skeletal man with burning black eyes and dirty, curly beard said breathlessly, 'Hastinapur? I have been there recently. You are . . . a *Kaurava*, a brother of Duryodhana?'

Karna felt a stab of irritation. He didn't want to be forced into giving specific details, especially to a mystic. 'No,' he replied. It was true, he consoled himself. Although an adopted brother, he was unrelated by blood to Duryodhana.

The mystic may have sensed Karna's reticence but that didn't stop him, 'You are of the royal court?'

'Yes,' said Karna abruptly.

'They say the royal court is . . . full of activity these days,' said the mystic with a suggestive smile.

Karna replied through gritted teeth, 'Royal courts are usually full of activities.'

The other mystic, a thicker man with an excess of coarse, henna-coloured hair and far less coyness than his companion, now chimed in, 'Yes, yes, but they say that the Hastinapur palace is busy looking for the Pandavas, who are in hiding!'

Karna gasped. The old sage spoke before he could say anything, 'The night is upon us. It will be beneficial if we retire to meditate on the day,' he paused, 'the minds of men are like rivers. As long as a river flows fast, it will encounter strong currents, rocks and rapids in its path. However, when the river slows to become still, that is when it is at its deepest and life can thrive in it.'

He spoke to Karna and the mystics, 'Our students will wait upon your requirements. Please have a pleasant sleep.' He stood up slowly and everyone else followed, hands folded and heads bowed.

Karna wasn't sure he wanted to stay on in the hermitage after what had just happened. He was on edge and the thought of spending a night next to those vile mystics was unpleasant to say the least. All were welcome in hermitages, beggar or prince alike, and for the first time, Karna wished they were a little more discriminating about the people they let inside their walls.

He went inside the hut he was directed towards and took a straw mat from the corner. Then, he went outside and laid it out in the open. As he lay on it, staring up at the stars and the almost full moon in the night sky, he wondered how the mystics knew about the desperate search for the Pandavas. It was a secret as far as he knew, confined within Duryodhana's close circle. Did the people really know about palace matters in such detail, he thought. Did they discuss among themselves how Duryodhana planned to track down the Pandavas and send them back into exile? And, if they did and even people like the mystics knew about it, then it was possible that the news had spread into other kingdoms and perhaps even the Pandavas themselves had heard of it. Karna felt uncomfortable, like a child caught doing something wrong.

Suddenly, he felt quiet footsteps coming towards him. He stiffened and his hand instinctively went towards his sword, sheathed by his side. The moonlight was quite bright tonight and he could see a blurry shape approach him from inside one of the huts. As it got closer, he recognised the thin mystic. What now, he thought angrily. He sat up, trying to look as daunting as he could in the darkness.

The mystic approached slowly, diffidently and knelt on his haunches next to Karna. He whispered, 'I can be of help to you, o' royal.'

Karna could smell a mixture of rotting deerskin, old sweat, smoky incense, *bhang* and stale betel nut on the man beside him. Revulsion gave way to anger, 'Get away from me, you dirty creature!' he growled softly.

'A moment of patience I beg of you, o' royal. You will thank me for it,' the man's smile was ingratiating.

'Speak your part quickly and be gone.'

The mystic spoke quickly, 'A piece of information I have, its value to you cannot be underestimated. I will relinquish it for a reward.'

Karna paused. What could this mystic tell him? 'What is it?'

'I know where the Pandavas are hiding,' the mystic said breathlessly.

Karna didn't believe a word, 'Really? Where?' he said with a sneer.

'A reward, sir. Please. For a poor man,' the mystic folded his hands and cupped them towards Karna in a begging gesture.

'Your reward will be that I don't kill you tonight in this forest,' Karna whispered harshly. Bribery or corruption of any sort was adharmic and repulsive to him. 'Or perhaps, I should kill you anyway, for vicious spreading of untruths is a crime in the eyes of the Gods.'

The mystics eyes widened. He had not expected this reaction. He eyed Karna's sword nervously, 'Prince, royal, you are merciful, you will be blessed with strong sons,' he whined, 'a small token ...'

'Get away from me,' Karna said as he jerked his body towards the mystic in an intimidating gesture, sending the man reeling backwards and falling on his back. He scampered back up on his haunches and took a few steps back. Now, he was scared. He folded his hands again, 'The kingdom of Matsya sir! They say Bhimsena, the Pandava, works as king Virata's cook!'

Karna's fingers felt his sword beside him as he asked, 'Where does your information come from?'

The mystic hesitated and then whimpered, 'The palace servants. They suspect it might be him ...'

Karna lunged towards the mystic and held his matted hair in one hand. With the other, he placed his sheathed sword on the man's neck. 'For this baseless, flighty gossip of servants you wake me and demand money? I should finish you off right now!'

'Mercy, prince, mercy!' the mystic whispered frantically.

'Get out of this hermitage right now before I make good my intention,' Karna threw the man away from himself and watched him scamper into the hut. A moment later, the two mystics hurriedly saw themselves out of the gates.

Karna watched them go with disgust. He had been harsh with the mystic but it had been for good reason. Not only was he condemning the man's corrupt behaviour but also sending out the message that Hastinapur had no intention of uncovering the Pandavas.

But could it be true? He wondered. If Bhimsena was working in disguise as King Virata's cook, then the others would not be far. He knew he should go and find out and, if what the mystic said is true, expose the Pandavas. Karna felt the same guilty unease he had experienced when Duryodhana had asked him to go on this mission. He shut his eyes and willed himself to sleep.

The next day, Karna set out towards the kingdom of Matsya, arriving in the bustling kingdom on a galloping Kali by twilight. He spent the night in a merchant's house, having rewarded him generously for his hospitality by gifting him with a thick gold chain from his own neck.

In the morning, he set out towards the palace dressed inconspicuously in the merchant's borrowed clothing, his jewelry and royal garb wrapped safely in linen on Kali's back. He didn't want to alert the king to his presence for, if he were to be formally received and the Pandavas were indeed, in the palace, they would surely flee.

He found out at the palace gate that the King and his courtiers had gone to the forest for an early morning hunt. A little delicate probing led to the information that the king was due to have his midday meal by the banks of the river, so his staff had set up an outdoor kitchen there.

Karna couldn't have asked for a better opportunity to find out if Bhimsena the Pandava was indeed disguised as the King's cook. He galloped to the river and then rode Kali up its bank, looking for the exact spot. He didn't have to wait long. In the distance, was the sight of an elaborate kitchen, with oversized pots cooking over three large fires and about forty men working around a large mass of food. They chopped, fried and steamed vegetables, ground spices and cleaned lentils. In one corner, the butchers cleaned bird, boar and deer meat and prepared it for the cooking. All the men progressed gingerly with their work, as if the king's arrival was imminent.

Karna tied Kali to a tree in the forest, out of sight. Then, covering his head with his white stole, as if to shield it from the sun, he began to walk towards the kitchen. He took care to walk in between the trees, so his presence was not detected until he was almost on the kitchen site.

Karna stood in one corner, behind the work horses, and looked around carefully. In the bustle, no one even noticed him. His gaze scanned everyone in sight until it halted on one man.

He was larger, much larger than the rest, towering over them by the measure of many hands. He was heavily built as well, corpulent of belly, but muscular of arms, neck and shoulders. These, he covered with a cook's cloth, his head modestly covered under a turban with the king's insignia. His moustache was short, as was customary among men of low rank but his head was held with a pride, an inborn nobility that made him stand out from those around him. Karna looked closer. The man's eyes were bright and alert, concentrated wholly on the job before him, a pot into which he stirred spices. His voice was low as he called out to his assistants, who ran back and forth with ingredients, but with the innate authority of one who has had servants since birth. Karna had encountered that voice many times before, the last time being in the court of Hastinapur thirteen years ago, where it had sworn to kill Duryodhana for humiliating Draupadi in open court. There was no mistaking it; this was Bhimsena, the Pandava.

Karna felt the rumblings of excitement in his stomach. He had to decide how to proceed. The appropriate thing to do would be to send word to Duryodhana in Hastinapur while he remained here in disguise, tracking the Pandavas. He wondered how Duryodhana would handle the information. He would probably arrive in Matsya and reveal the Pandavas in dramatic style with King Virata as witness. He would then command the Pandavas to restart their next thirteen-year exile immediately and force them back into the forest. Karna frowned. He felt extremely uneasy once more. Dharma, surely would be violated with that course of action. What would be the right thing to do, he questioned himself.

After a few moments of pondering the answer to his question, Karna did what came naturally to him. Never one to skulk or stand in the shadows, he walked forward to face his enemy and confront him.

Bhimsena saw him walk towards him and recognition lit up his eyes immediately. For an instant, Karna thought that Bhimsena might bolt and run but then an obstinate, bullish look came into his eyes and he squared his shoulders, prepared to face Karna.

'Good day, o' cook,' said Karna softly as he stood in front of Bhimsena.

A moment of confusion in Bhimsena's eyes and then he said, 'Good day to you. Would you like words with me?'

'Only if I do not take you away from your work,' replied Karna.

'Follow me.' Bhimsena led Karna into the forest trees and stopped when they were out of earshot. Then, he turned and said, 'What have you to say?'

Karna didn't know, but after a moment he said, 'You have been discovered, o' Bhimsena. Your brothers and wife must be close by as well and it will not take long to find them out.'

Bhimsena grit his teeth and flexed his muscles in anger. His eyes were ablaze, 'If I kill you, then no discovery has been made.'

Karna felt a wave of pleasure. Words of battle. This was more to his taste, 'I will not give you an easy fight. And, what of your fellow cooks over there? If they see you as a warrior, your disguise will be uncovered soon enough.'

Bhimsena realised the truth of this, so he stood, undecided, gnawing his lip and clenching his fists. Both men faced each other, opponents who couldn't fight except with their eyes.

Bhimsena spoke first, 'Fight me like a man, o' Karna, on the battlefield. Kill me if you must, but at least do it with honour.'

Karna kept silent.

Bhimsena continued, 'To defeat me like this would be a coward's victory and you know it. I know Duryodhana is a coward, but I never thought you ...'

'Another word and I will cut your throat,' Karna whispered with violence.

'... were a lowly coward as well.'

Karna lunged at Bhimsena's throat, who caught his hands in his own. They locked their arms together, pushing and wrestling one another until Bhimsena had Karna, the smaller of the two, backed against a tree. Then he pushed away, breathing heavily and spat at Karna, 'Maybe, revealing us is the only way you can win. Perhaps, you should take your chance, coward!'

Karna made to lunge at Bhimsena again but something stopped him. The other cooks were beginning to stare at them from the clearing. In an instant, he knew what he had to do. He strode up to Bhimsena and looked him in the eyes, 'You will die for calling me a coward, Pandava! Carry on with your charade until the finish of the exile period and keep your heads low, for in the end we shall meet on the battlefield and I will make you answer for today.'

Bhimsena stood still, looking confused, 'You will not reveal us?'

'I will not,' Karna replied, fire in his eyes.

'Duryodhana will want us back in the forest,' said Bhimsena as if he couldn't believe it.

'Duryodhana will fight you with honour, as will I.' Karna gathered his stole, which had fallen during their tussle, and covered his head once more, 'Heed my words, o' Bhimsena and tell your brothers as well. I swear, I will not reveal your whereabouts for I shall wait and relish the day we can fight, man to man, on a field of battle. On that day I shall kill you and your brothers.'

Bhimsena stared at Karna in disbelief for a few moments. Then, he smiled with pleasure and anticipation, 'I look forward to that day as well. And, in return for your silence, o' Karna, I hereby vow that, though I shall annihilate your army and kill all your adopted brothers, starting with Duryodhana, I will spare your life.'

'I don't ask nor expect such pointless mercy on your part, Pandava. I leave now,' Karna turned and began to walk away.

Bhimsena called out softly after him, 'I have your word?'

Karna continued walking without turning, 'You have my silence.'

www.ingramcontent.com/pod-product-compliance
Lightning Source LLC
Chambersburg PA
CBHW020206090426
42734CB00008B/961

9 788129 114464